On The Side Of Angels

*The life story of Gordon Higginson
compiled by
Jean Bassett*

Tudor Press (London),
27 Old Gloucester Street,
London WC1N 3XX.

First published 1993

© Jean Bassett

All rights reserved. No portion of this book may be reproduced or utilised in any form or by any means, electronic or mechanical, including photocopying or retrieval system, without the prior permission in writing of the publisher. Nor is it to be otherwise circulated in any form or binding or cover other than that in which it is presented.

This book is sold subject to the Standard Conditions of Sale of Net Books and may not be re-sold in the United Kingdom below the net price fixed by the publishers for the book.

ISBN 1 874514 05 4

Printed and bound by the Longdunn Press Ltd, Barton Manor, St Philips, Bristol BS2 0RL.

Dedication

To my sister Hazel, my niece Gillian and my sister-in-law Elsie for all the help they have given to me over the years.

— Gordon Higginson

In Memorium

Gordon Higginson passed to the spirit world on January 18, 1993, just four days after making final corrections to "On The Side Of Angels." He passed suddenly at his home in Longton, Staffs.

As both a medium and President of the Spiritualists' National Union, Gordon championed and served the spirit world unstintingly for decades.

Both the publisher and author would like to wish him well in the Higher Life and express their gratitude for his help and co-operation in making "On The Side of Angels" possible.

It is a fitting memorial to one who was a giant not only amongst men but mediums as well.

—Jean Bassett, author.
Tony Ortzen, Tudor Press (London).

CONTENTS

Chapter	Page
INTRODUCTION	5
1 MY MOTHER	8
2 FAMILY GUIDANCE	12
3 ARE YOU CALLING ME?	14
4 CIRCLE DEVELOPMENT	19
5 TRANCE	22
6 GOING TO WAR	29
7 TRAINING FOR LIFE	37
8 POST WAR YEARS	44
9 FORMS MATERIALISE	52
10 SPIRIT PROMISE KEPT	59
11 TV OR NOT TV?	71
12 ANIMALS AND THE AFTERLIFE	74
13 TRAINING MEDIUMS	76
14 MY GREATEST LOVE	89
15 A WHITE ELEPHANT?	97
16 GETTING GOOD EVIDENCE	108
17 TO UNITE ALL PEOPLES	114
18 SEEING THE DEAD	120
19 SPIRIT DIRECTION	130
20 POLL PROVES IT	138
21 I AM ACCUSED	153
22 MOTHER RETURNS	160
23 SPIRITUALISM SHOWS THE WAY	169
24 APPARITIONS	180
25 THE MEDIA	189
26 MINISTRY OF HEALING	193
27 AS I SEE IT	201
28 THERE IS NO END	208

INTRODUCTION

I SUPPOSE the story of my life began when my mother was 14 years of age. My birth was ordained! My mother, Fanny, was told by the spirit world years before she was married that I would be a medium and have important work to do here on this earth. Even I do not always understand why this should be with some people, but I do know that it was so with me. I also know that Spirit were right. Everything came to pass...just as they said it would.

And so long before my birth, my destiny was determined. Spirit foretold this to my mother. Although this first little story is to do with my mother coming into Spiritualism, it is also how I, too, came into Spiritualism before my mother met my father.

Mother was taken to a Spiritualist church when she was 14 years of age. Her aunt was Mrs Taylor, who started the first Spiritualist church in Blackpool, Lancs. She took Mother one afternoon to Longton Spiritualist Church, Staffs, to hear a medium work.

After a while this medium came to Mother and described a woman in great detail. One outstanding feature was a mark on her face, a mole about the size of a silver threepenny piece.

She went on to say: "This lady is named Fanny. She tells me that you are named after her." My mother said: "You are quite correct. That is my mother — but she is living, and is not passed. We left her at home to come here!"

"No, my dear. Your mother has passed away while you've been sitting here," said the medium. "You had to come here today because it was necessary for you to receive this evidence. You will one day stand here where I am and have a son who will follow you. Your name will be linked with this church for over one hundred years. And, during this time, this church will be successful."

Well my mother said, "No." She refused the message, and was in tears as she ran home. There she found that while she and her aunt had been at the church, her mother passed into Spirit: it had indeed been she who made her return that afternoon at Longton. It was this remarkable visitation from Spirit that changed my mother's life.

Mother went back to speak with the medium, whose husband was the president of the church. The medium was Annie Brittain, one of the most famous trance mediums in the country. She took my mother and trained her and also trained her aunt. My mother had always seen spirit people, but didn't really know before what it was all about. In fact, she had only ever told her aunt about it. Now they were both trained by this famous medium.

At that same time, another medium was being trained in Longton, Lilian Bailey, who went on to become a famous trance medium. Lilian's parents owned the Crown and Anchor Hotel in Longton. Annie Brittain trained many of these great mediums as well as being a fine trance medium herself.

My mother was a medium when she and my father married. She commenced working as a medium after four years of development and took her first service at Longton when she was 18. My father was not a Spiritualist, but she told him that she must remain a Spiritualist and medium. She did not ask him to be one, but knew by the earlier prophecy that she must continue with her spiritual work.

Mother said her children must know about her religion, which was Spiritualism, but that they would also know about my father's religion. We were brought up to know both Spiritualism and Christianity.

The first child born to my parents was a boy so my mother thought this was the son that was to be a medium. He was taken to Longton church to be named. The second child was also a boy so my mother thought, "Well, it has to be one or the other." He was also taken along to the church to be named. Then came a girl so my mother and my father decided that three children were enough.

When, nearly three years later, they realised I was on the way they were not very pleased, but along I came. And it was me that was to be the medium! My two brothers and sister have no mediumistic powers.

Now the wonder of this is that my mother had been told at the age of 14 she would stand on Longton platform, and that she would have a son who would follow her. Mother stayed at Longton church as their medium for 70 years. I took my first Spiritualist service at Longton as a medium when I was 12 years old and so together we have spanned over a century of time. As long as I am connected with Longton church, so will my mother be linked.

There was nothing the matter with my mother's mother when they went to the church that afternoon. There was no reason to suppose for one moment she was about to pass, but she had a sudden heart attack. This was just in time, you could say, to give such marvellous evidence to mother to show her the way forward. Not just for her but also, you see, for me. This shows that mediums are coming into the world not by mistake, but through the influence of a higher mind which is in charge of things.

Christianity was founded on two visitations of Spirit. One was to Mary, who was told that she was to have a son and would name him Jesus. The other was to Joseph, who was told to marry Mary. Throughout the history of this world there have always been visitations of angels.

Chapter 1

MY MOTHER

I KNOW that my mother was aware of her imminent departure from this life and knew she wanted me with her. We had spent so much time together. She did not completely trust the doctor's ability to tell when the spirit actually separated from the body, but knew that I, as a medium trained by herself, would know.

My mother was determined I should be there and told me so. She was always a very determined woman — and I knew she would have things her way.

I had to curtail my spiritual and daily work while she was ill because one of the family had to be with her at all times. I had taken time to go to our shop, in which my niece Gillian, her husband Frank, my sister Hazel and I were all partners. There were so many things that had to be seen to so I snatched time when I could. But I was no sooner there than the phone went. I was to come home at once.

Seeing me, my mother seemed to relax. "I am so tired," she sighed. "I really want to go. The time has come." And so it had. She smiled, quit the body she had occupied for 88 years and peacefully went home. My mother's friend Kath and I held her hands while her spirit left the body.

It was a beautiful passing. It was a very emotional experience, but I knew it was right for her. My mother had worked so hard in this life; she was going to friends and loved ones. Physically, I had now lost my dearest companion, my mother.

Mother was a wonderful medium. I think she was the best that I have ever known; she was my mentor, tutor and critic. She would stand no nonsense on the platform and expected the highest of standards of work both from herself and those around her. She is still remembered by many who she helped by her mediumship.

Although she did not work so much in her latter years, my mother gave the occasional sitting when it was needed. She had absolute trust in the accuracy of her link with the spirit world.

Once, some six years before her passing, she agreed to see a young woman and her mother.

Marjorie Hackney had lost her father. She and her mother needed the comfort of knowing that their loved one was well and happy, and that he had recovered from his tragic passing. Having given that assurance through the evidence presented, Mother brought through another communicator, a young boy called Anthony who was known to Marjorie, although not a relative.

Anthony spoke of a rose which his father had taken from the funeral flowers. This was not an unusual occurrence: the rose would kept in remembrance until it had withered and then be buried in the garden. What was unusual was that a year afterwards, a rose bush started to grow in that spot in a garden where there were no other roses. Anthony spoke of this and predicted that the bush would bloom. Marjorie checked up on this statement. And sure enough, six perfect buds were waiting to bloom.

Mother gave such wonderful detail, but was never afraid to be controversial. Spirit frequently approached her in the most unusual ways. Once she was at the cinema and became very aware of a hymn sung throughout the film, "Sweet Spirit, hear my prayer." She had never heard it before, but the day after a woman called at the house selling hymn sheets; there was the hymn, "Sweet Spirit."

A few hours later she attended the Spiritualist church and, as she was singing the self-same hymn, became aware that a spirit entity had moved in close behind her. She told me the story.

"I felt as though something sharp was being driven into my chest," she said. "I shouted, 'No, don't kill me!'" The spirit manifested and identified himself as Major Bailey.

Later the spirit recounted that he had killed his wife, but his body was now lying entangled with a boat under the Serpentine in London.

Well, Mother made inquiries. Major Bailey was indeed wanted for the murder of his wife, and was thought to have joined the Foreign Legion.

At a later sitting, the major was able to describe the exact location of his body. When the area was searched, it was recovered from under the boat where it was, indeed, being mutilated, as described by the dead man. The distress the major felt at the mutilation of his physical remains was eased. He was able to move on mentally from that to make his natural spiritual progression, to work out his salvation.

We so often forget that spirit people are subject to difficulties and sometimes need help before they can move forward. Mother made communication look so simple.

Once she told a woman who had come to be comforted on the loss of her husband that it was not he who had passed; another man had been buried in his place. With her usual courage she had not doubted the truth of spirit information.

The woman went away confused as my mother's reputation was well-known, but there was no other hint that her husband had survived. Her grieving process had been interrupted, but this very fact helped her to accept the later appearance of her still living husband and to welcome him without the guilt she would otherwise have felt in prematurely assuming his death.

However, Mother was not the most tactful medium in the world, but she cared; she cared about the major. She knew he would have to compensate for his earthly crime, but accepted that he needed to clear his obsession about his physical body before he could start on the more important task of putting things right which he had done wrong.

No, Mother really cared about the people, Spiritualist and non-Spiritualist, who flocked to her home to receive the help she could give. She cared about her family; she cared and worried about me.

Deep within her own feelings, Mother did not want me to be a medium because she knew the problems I would have to face having experienced so many of the hurts that people inflict upon workers for Spirit. She knew that if I pursued my chosen road I, too, would have to go through these experiences and even more. Actually, Mother wanted me to be a minister, but not of the Spiritualists' National Union. That was not her ambition for me, but she realised and accepted my destiny and was fierce in my defence when I needed it. It hurt her when I was hurt. She always wanted to protect me in that way.

My very dear friend Eric Hatton, currently vice-president of the SNU, conducted her funeral service. It could not have been easy for him because he was so close to Mother, almost like a son.

There wasn't enough room for all the people who wanted to come so we had to arrange another service. The funeral director said he had never seen so many flowers. There were so many letters and telegrams from all over the world. Even now, flowers arrive at our church for her anniversary. People still remember her.

I am not ashamed to say I grieved. I love my mother and still miss her earthly presence. I know she will be there when I go over, probably ready to tell me how I could have done things better!

Chapter 2

FAMILY GUIDANCE

THERE is purpose to many of our lives. I believe we have a part to play. We don't come here by mistake: many of us have a mission in life. From her early experience, my mother became not just a medium, but a very great medium. She was ready for when I, the youngest, showed signs of the power of Spirit. My mother guarded, guided, protected and encouraged me ready for the work that I would one day have to do.

The link between my mother and myself became very important and close because of the mediumistic side of our natures. My father never became a practising Spiritualist, as such, but gave up his religion to look after us so that my mother could continue with her work. We spent a lot of time together at the weekends when mother was travelling.

Father never wanted me to be a medium: he could see that it took so much out of a person's life and wanted me to have the freedom to enjoy a more normal life. I did not take much to sport. Mother tended to protect me from the rougher elements in life, but I did play tennis and basketball which I think pleased them.

Mother knew that I had a Spiritualist future because of the prophecy and that she must prepare me for it.

She had accepted an obligation, a responsibility. Of course, all my family supported me in their own ways. I was the baby of the family — and they loved me! They knew there was something special about me spiritually, but also spoiled me as the youngest in the family.

One of my earliest memories of spirit communication was with my grandmother. I was talking to her when my mother came in. She asked who I was talking to. I told her that it was a lady. My mother said to me, "Describe her." I did so mentioning a mole. "What is her name?" asked Mother. Well, the spirit lady didn't give the name, but said Mother was named after her which was, of course, exactly the way that Annie Brittain had given the evidence to my mother all those years before!

I have the same mole as my grandmother on my face, not as large but in exactly the same place. Of course, this confirmed that I was the one that would be the medium. Years later I took a friend named George Mitchell to see Annie Brittain. The sitting was booked in his name. Annie had not seen me since I was four years old. I was 26 at the time. There was no way of her knowing who I was.

It was a double sitting so we went in together. Annie went into trance. The guide came through and said that my friend, George, was not a Spiritualist and that the sitting should be for me, not him, because I was a medium. The guide also went on to say that she knew my mother. This was true: my mother did know Annie's spirit guide. She gave me the most wonderful evidence.

Annie asked afterwards if it was accurate: she still didn't realise who I was until I told her my name. Then, of course, she remembered.

My army friend, George, did receive remarkable evidence about his father, who had passed away before the war, even to the uniform he had worn years previously. I did not know this. Annie Brittain could not possibly have known. It was very convincing for him.

Chapter 3

ARE YOU CALLING ME?

I DO not have many early memories of spirit people, but do remember the clear vision of my friend Cuckoo. She was, of course, a spirit friend. That was not her name: it was the way I called to her, then she would call back. Because of this she chose to be called Cuckoo. She has been with me ever since and become quite famous.

I remember once when I was ill and had some time off school I was having difficulties in doing my work. Cuckoo had always talked to me and often used to come with me to school. I couldn't do my work because I had missed so much and so I asked Cuckoo.

She helped me by giving me answers when I needed them. I suppose it was cheating, but it didn't seem like that at the time. Unfortunately, she didn't tell me how she worked out the answers — and the teachers were suspicious. They could see that the answers were right, but wanted to know how I was getting them because they knew I couldn't do the work.

My mother had to go to the school to explain. My father wouldn't go. "No," he said. "This is your fault and you must deal with it. You are the medium. Gordon takes after you...and you are answerable to it!" Father didn't really approve of my mediumship, although he did not argue with my mother; very few did really! Mother had a talk to me. I told her about Cuckoo, but wasn't allowed to ask my friend to do my work for me after that. I don't know what Mother said to my teachers, but they must have understood because they were not cross after she had been to see them.

Cuckoo was like a school friend really. Mother used to ask, "What is she like?" I would say, "Well she is just like us really, except that she has a black face."

We had a good life. Although we were not affluent, we never went without. One thing we always had were music lessons. Mother was a musician herself and made sure we were properly trained. I had the ability to hear things once and then just sit down and play them through. I was very gifted that way, but as soon as I started to develop my mediumistic powers my musical ability fell away.

I did not lose it for I still play from time to time, but my mind was on other things and they took precedence. I feel that the musical gift was tied in with my mediumistic ability, but had made my choice; or was it made before I ever arrived here on earth? I also had singing and elocution lessons for my voice. I knew it had to be used during my life's work so it was important that it should be right.

I found I was quite popular with people. I was used to being made a lot of at home being the baby of the family and, of course, all my mother's friends used to spoil me. I had many friends at school and where I lived, but also belonged to the Lyceum — the Spiritualist Sunday School — so had friends there as well. Through this I mixed with other children who had interests in the spirit world so never thought that my gift was strange.

After all these years some of these friends these still come to Longton church to see me work. I was a very lucky person to be surrounded by so much love. Several of my school friends' families attended the Spiritualist church. They would talk about me and then my friends would question me about Spiritualism. In the classroom they would send little notes along, saying things like: "Can you see anyone? Are there any ghosts here?" I rather enjoyed that because it made me feel important.

The teachers knew I was mediumistic, especially when I was about nine or ten and others were starting to realise about my gifts. The were quite good about it really, and I got on quite well with them. It was not easy sometimes to be a medium and a child, but it could have been a lot worse.

Many people, knowing that my training took up so much of my young life, have asked me if I regret all the things I missed, if I resented all the hours spent in development. I took it all for granted. It was the life that I had. I knew no different and had many privileges.

My middle brother and sister went to the same school so we used to walk there and back together. I was not very good at religious studies because I was rather confused. I belonged to the Lyceum and had lessons there on Sundays which often seemed to contradict what I was being taught in the school. I always liked history and art and, of course, music. Mother insisted that we all pay attention to our lessons and our homework. We couldn't get away with anything with her; she was a disciplinarian. Very loving, but quite strict.

Our house was always full of not just my friends but those of my brothers and sisters. Mother was so intelligent: she taught us to like school and learning. I would have liked to have gone on to university, but that was not to be. I did take shorthand and typing, and went to Wolverhampton Technical College after the war. Father was a much quieter person than Mother, but was a very important member of our family; always there! That is very important to children — to know that their parents are there for them.

I had a good childhood. Mother was always baking for us. If she saw someone in the street who was hungry, she would feed them. I have seen her put down a mattress for a stranger who had nowhere to sleep.

Of course, it would be a bit more difficult — possibly dangerous — to do that these days, but then you could help people safely. My father supported her in everything that she wanted to do. We didn't have luxuries, but we had a happy home life.

Seeing spirit has always been so natural to me. I can remember seeing many spirit people and not being able to differentiate at the time as to whether they were from earth or the spirit world. My mother, being a medium, was able to understand so this was not a difficulty for me. Because it was so natural, like speaking or breathing, I have no idea when my gift first showed itself. Perhaps the first momentous communication was with my Grandmother. I didn't understand death: the people that spoke to me were so real! Fortunately, Mother knew how to handle and teach me.

I suppose I have been a very fortunate person in as much as

my childhood was a very good one, having a very wonderful mother and a very understanding father, but above all being raised knowing what Spiritualism really is.

I remember my mother taking me to Blackpool when I was a boy: this would be in the early 1930s. I would be about ten or eleven. It was to see a relative of my mother's who was also a very fine medium. In fact, I believe she was responsible for the very first meeting ever to be held in Blackpool. I didn't know at that time, but they had been trained together by Annie Brittain at Longton.

Each week my great-aunt took a room over Yates Wine Bar and conducted the service herself. It was so popular that you had to queue for quite a long time to get in. My mother wanted me to meet her aunt, Mrs Taylor, because she wished to ask advice on my own development. I thought at first she was rather old and a bit peculiar, but was soon to change my mind.

Mother could see that her aunt was not too well that day and offered to take the meeting, but her suggestion was refused. "I will take the meeting even if I am dying!" she declared. The ladies in my family tended to speak their minds! I still feel privileged to have watched and seen what a wonderful response she got, the way in which she handled the people who were packed right down the stairs.

During the demonstration, she stated there was a gentleman at the bottom of the stairs who must be brought up as his wife in Spirit wanted to speak to him. She gave his name. There was quite a commotion outside. Eventually, a man came into the room looking tired and wet from the rain. "You didn't know that you were coming here tonight," said my great-aunt. "No," he replied. "I was only sheltering in the doorway to keep out of the rain."

"Well," said she. "Your wife knew you were there. She has only passed away recently and wishes me to give you a message of hope and comfort. She tells me I must come down off this platform and to feel in your coat pocket for you have something in there that she wishes you to destroy."

The gentleman seemed to be amazed by this and moved to leave. My great-aunt told the people around him to prevent him from leaving. She approached him...and took from his pocket a small bottle. It was a bottle of poison!

"You were thinking of taking your own life because you have lost your wife," she said, "but she does not want you to join her yet. You have work to do and must carry on. Promise me that you will not even think of such a thing again." The man broke down in tears. The promise was given!

What an experience it was to be there and to hear such outstanding evidence of life after death. To think not just about the actual message, but the work by Spirit behind the scenes; to have arranged for the man to take shelter in just the right doorway at the right time so his wife could, through my great-aunt, save him from taking his own life. I do not know, of course, but I imagine that person's life must have changed after that valuable experience.

Spiritualism isn't about dying: it is about living. Spiritualism is not working with lower forces: it is about working with God. When we see and hear these experiences, we realise that there is a Divine force which permeates the whole.

We see in these experiences a God answering prayer. We also see what can be done for people who have no knowledge or faith in Spiritualism when they come a great crisis in their life. God can answer prayer, but not alone, only with the help of other people who are channels.

I wanted to share this because although it happened so long ago things like this are occurring all the time. Why then all the prejudice? Why do people pull Spiritualism to pieces? Of course, we have black sheep in our number, but we have many who are doing wonderful things for others, to help them to have the strength to go on with this life in spite of their difficulties. It is these experiences which make Spiritualism great.

Chapter 4

CIRCLE DEVELOPMENT

I WILL always remember my first circle because I was too small to sit in a chair so they had to find a stool for me. I felt so important sitting with the grown ups.

My mother would ask everyone else what they had seen or felt but not me! On one occasion I said, "Why are you asking everyone else and not me?" "One of the first things you must learn," she said, "is discipline and obedience. When I think you are ready, then I will ask you."

For the first 12 months I was not allowed to do or say anything. Later on I was able to stand up to say what I had seen, heard or felt. This would have been when I was five or six. It was not until later that I was allowed to talk about my experiences in the development circle. Subsequently, I was in two circles. My mother was the teacher in both. One, as I have said, was a developing circle.

In this, I practised psychometry and also clairvoyance where I was blindfolded so I could not see. Sometimes I had to work when I could neither see nor hear. This developed my spiritual sense, the sense which functions separately from the five senses. I had to work very hard and be very patient. My mother would pull the message to pieces, but I had to accept this and then make sense of it. I look back and see how important this development was in my work.

My brothers and sister all sat in Mother's home circle. Her guide would come through after she went into trance and talk to us. This was an experience we took very much for granted at the time. It was not until many years later I knew how privileged I had been and how much I learnt from this early contact with Spirit. They conveyed so much love and gave us so much help in our development.

I took my first meeting on my twelfth birthday. My mother gave it to me as a surprise. She had bought me a new pair of trousers and a white shirt and sports jacket so I felt so very smart. But when Mother told me I was going to share the platform with her it was the greatest present anyone could ever have given me. I was so longing to start working and sure I would do well. When the meeting was over I expected only praise, but Mother realised I still needed to go back to working in circle and expanding my gift. I did take bookings, but always with my mother.

Mother only allowed me to be on platform about 20 minutes. She taught me not to waste power or the gift, not to overdo it and to control my emotions. My mediumship owes a great deal to the discipline of that early training.

I became a boy medium when I was 12 years old and travelled with my mother and a speaker. I had been trained as a demonstrator so needed a speaker to go with me. My mother worked to develop my mediumship to the calibre she felt was necessary. There were, at that time, about a dozen girl and boy mediums working on the various platforms throughout the country. There were some very fine workers. That era seemed to end as we grew older and has not returned. I think that this is a pity. It means people are starting to train at an older age.

Perhaps this is because of the changes in social conditions; people stay at school much longer and study harder so don't start training as mediums at the early age. Now, there are no longer the child workers. As far as I was concerned, I had to cope with my school work, my music practice and spiritual training in the week because I was travelling to take services at the weekend.

These days, the authorities would probably frown on parents who allowed their child to work so hard. And it was hard in some ways, but I think that we, who did work in this way, had a very special childhood. It was not the same as others, but we had Spirit with us and that gave us so much.

I became known before the war for giving full names and addresses. This was considered quite remarkable and widely reported in the papers in the towns where I worked as well as the

Spiritualist publications. Actually, what happened was that my mother watched one of my demonstrations and thought I could do better.

She undertook to give me further training. Mother bandaged my eyes and stopped up my ears so I couldn't hear or see anything around me except that which came from the spirit world. There were no distractions. No clues were given by the recipient of the message that I could use, consciously or otherwise. She then took me into a group and asked me to demonstrate without being able to see or hear anything but Spirit.

In this way, I learned to become fully aware of the spirit people around me. At other times, Mother would ask me questions like: "Where do you think they live? What does the house look like?" It was quite surprising really what results I started to get just by learning to ask for more detail.

Then, of course, I became known for this type of work. I spent about two years developing in this way with Mother taking notes so she could check afterwards to see how accurate I was. It is necessary to concentrate on the Spirit and not on the person who is getting the message. Anything like this helps the medium to get closer links with the spirit world.

Before the war, I worked anywhere within easy reach of Stoke. We went by bus because we didn't have a car. I always worked with my mother at first. When I was going wrong or couldn't get any more she would just say to me, "My son, it is my turn now." If I had been wrong, she was so kind: she would never say anything to me in front of people. She waited until we were on the bus on the way home and then let me have it! Mother always insisted I should prove my links. This encouraged me to work harder.

In those days, we worked with a separate speaker. I didn't do the speaking at first because it was not really my thing. Sometimes Mother took the speaking, but there were others. Mr Hand was an excellent speaker. Then there was Mr Brock. I worked with some very fine people and took note of the ways in which they handled the people because I realised this was an important part of platform presentation.

Chapter 5

TRANCE

I REALISED quite early on that I was a trance medium. There occurred a situation which was quite unexpected and I was going to say accidental, but, of course, looking at the circumstances it is obvious that Spirit engineered the whole thing.

When I was 18, I was booked to take the demonstration of clairvoyance at a Sunday service to be held at the Hanley Spiritualist Church in the Potteries. I was asked by the chairlady if I would also take the address as the speaker had not arrived. I refused, as I was not a speaker, but had trained only as a clairvoyant. I said to Mrs Northall that I was sure she would be able to give the address. A dedicated Salvationist before becoming a Spiritualist, I felt she could speak on how she converted. Mrs Northall agreed.

Hanley was a fine church, with a strong congregation and an old fashioned-type pulpit. I took my place as the service started and during the hymn felt very tired. I decided, as the speaker took the invocation, that I would shut my eyes for a moment. People expected the medium to shut their eyes from time to time either in prayer or preparation for the service. I decided no one would realise because I was hidden by the sides of the pulpit. I shut my eyes feeling so drowsy — and knew no more.

The next thing I knew was that the chairlady stood by my side offering me a glass of water. I thought I had fainted, apologised and said to her, "Am I to give the demonstration now?" "Yes, after we have sung the hymn," came the reply. I asked if the address had gone all right. "But you gave the address!" said Mrs Northall.

Of course, I told her that I couldn't have done as I didn't do the speaking. She explained I had given an excellent trance address, and moved down the steps from the pulpit among the people. The spirit control had then given those present a message to be given to me, the medium, when I came out of trance.

The message was for my mother. It stated she was to find an envelope in which would be found the name of the spirit control, Light, and that this was also my the spirit name. I had never heard of any letter being kept and was a little nervous about telling mother I had gone into trance.

She did not want me to develop trance as she felt it should come later in life. I was only young and had a job of work as well as my spiritual work to cope with. Mother thought it would be too much for me. I gathered up my courage and told her what had happened.

I rather expected a telling off, but instead she went off to her room and came back with a sealed envelope. Inside was a paper written by Annie Brittain at the time of my naming — the Spiritualist alternative to Christening — and kept all these years. Of course, the name on that paper was Light!

At the time of my naming, Mrs Brittain had refused to give my Spirit name to anyone, but wrote it down and stated: "One day this child will give you this name himself. For a remarkable experience and revelation will take place which will confirm to you what you have been told about the spiritual destiny of this child." That guide, named 18 years before at the time of my naming and confirmed in the trance address as Light, has been with me ever since. I could only accept that this remarkable revelation showed there was indeed a spiritual part of my life for which I was born to fulfil.

The medium who was to have taken the speaking came into the church at the end of the service, Mr Brock, an excellent demonstrator who was most reliable and had travelled to this church many times before. That night he got on the wrong bus, ended up miles away and had taken all this time getting to the church. Was the situation manipulated by the spirit world? One wonders if they were behind it to give me this experience where I would be introduced to the guide who would work with me in the future.

Of course, after this I spent even more effort to develop the spiritual side of my life. I made it the priority. Although I had found no difficulty with that first experience of trance, I did not find the next time nearly so easy. In fact, it was several years before I was able to demonstrate it properly. There were other factors which intervened with my development at that time. I was conscripted expecting to do six months, but as war had broken out I ended up doing over six years.

Although I accepted that I had the ability, I do not think I truly recognised the importance of this type of mediumship until just after the war when I needed unbiased advice from Spirit and my mother offered to give me this. She was able to do this only because she herself was an excellent trance worker. I had no doubts as to her integrity: do not think that. But I knew what she felt was right for me. I also knew that this was not what I wanted. Mother cared deeply for me and had very definite opinions which could not help but influence what she was receiving from Spirit in the ordinary way.

I believe that every genuine medium is a potential trance worker. If you are truly in touch with Spirit influences, then you need to bring that influence closer into your life. When people say they are natural mediums, all too often they mean they can see what they see, but do not depend upon the spirit to see it! I would contradict that and say that you cannot work without Spirit influence. If you are a mere psychic, then you don't have this quality. You are not a medium. All mediums possess powers of value that can be used by Spirit.

When a good medium is working, they lose themselves in the demonstration. They likewise lose all sense of time and often do not even hear the chairman saying that the time is up. The spirit world is giving us this experience which we can develop into a deeper state of trance.

Mediums will very often see the first signs of this when giving their address: the power takes over and they find themselves saying things that are not necessarily their own opinions. The knowledge is there, but the spirit world imposes a strong influence upon what is said. At the end of this there is often a feeling of being like a wet rag. In the past all mediums developed trance before they developed their mediumship into clairvoyance and clairaudience.

It is never too late. A lot of people go on for years then find that something is happening: they are feeling the power of spirit and the take over that happens in a trance state. At certain times in your life, your mediumship will change and you find yourself involved in things that you didn't imagine would be possible; changes take place, but only when you are ready for that experience.

I do think that a lot of people still have a fear of trance. They worry about what is happening, what is going on. They worry particularly about the unconscious state and who will be working through them and if it will be right. What they must realise is that like attracts like. In Spiritualism that is particularly true. It is important to develop this gift properly so that a trust is built up between the medium and the Spirit workers. If this is established, then there will be no fear.

We do know that certain mediums have tremendous powers, but do not use these powers to effect. The Spirit, the power, is always with them. What is not realised is that if they were a better channel then that power could be used properly. The Spirit will stay with them even though they are not being properly used because they have chosen that person to work with, hoping perhaps that they will be able to achieve great things with the power they hold. What goes wrong sometimes is that the person is not in keeping with the Spirit power who is with them.

I had a friend, George Bailey, who was a first class psychic. He would give people evidence — and was always right. My mother trained him and tried to persuade him to go into trance. George refused: he didn't want to see the spirit world and was quite afraid.

Gradually, my mother persuaded George into her circle. He used to go to sleep, but my mother never told him that this was a trance situation. The guides told us he was terrified of death! They manifested in his consciousness, but he wouldn't recognise them properly.

George was a boy medium. Indeed, until he was eighteen he was still billed as the boy medium. He was a marvellous medium. I believe this was because of the help my mother gave in his development. She trained him to be what a true medium is, a channel for the Spirit.

Lilian Nutter used to have a man control. At the age of twelve, she would go into trance and a mature man's voice emerged. It was fascinating to see and hear. Later she later became a remarkable transfiguration medium. In those years nearly every medium was a trance medium. They came under the power of the Spirit. The state of trance should be developed by all potential mediums first.

I believe this form of mediumship has a very important place in the future of Spiritualism. It is very evidential. I think there are many who have the ability, but don't recognise this.

The first thing that anyone training to develop trance must recognise is that it involves a change in personality. In the early stages they must not be afraid if they realise they are aware of what is going on. This is a fairly common mistake. People think they must be in the unconscious state for it to be genuine. This is not true: they will start in the semi-conscious state, but the unconscious will come later.

It is a very personal thing. People must learn to sit quietly, alone with their guides. They are best in a very small group, spending time alone in contemplation and feeling close to their guides. I used to love being alone with my mine.

But there are pitfalls. You cannot have just anybody sitting with you. You must check to make sure they are the right sort of person you want. It is not how many you have sitting, but the quality of those who are there.

They should have knowledge for the guidance given during the development, and should never eat for at least two or three hours before. It is not a good idea to have your stomach churning over as the relaxation which is a necessity for such development cannot take place. The body, soul and spirit must come together so deep breathing is vital.

When developing trance, you must learn breathing techniques. The actual way that you sit helps this. If you sit just any old how, then your shoulders are not straight and the chest is not able to expand properly. Sitting in an easy chair is useless as you will just go to sleep. You must learn to go into the quiet and let yourself sink into the vibrations in harmony with your breathing and with Spirit.

I must finish this chapter with a marvellous story which demonstrates two things. The first is what we have been speaking about: that the medium does not know what the guide does, but can be influenced even when in the conscious state.

The second is the wonderful co-operation which can exist between the people who are in Spirit. We tend to think of communication as being our prerogative between their world and ours, but my story shows clearly how they communicate with each other, something that is often forgotten.

Once I asked if I could take my mother to one of the Silver Birch seances. The guide of Maurice Barbanell who edited "Psychic News" for years and years, Silver Birch was one of the best ever spirit teachers. I duly wrote to Barbie, as friends called him, and a date was fixed. Mother had always wanted to share in the wonderful experience of talking with Silver Birch.

We set off by car and had to keep stopping because my mother couldn't sit for very long. Then fog came down and I started to panic. The Silver Birch circles always started on time at 7 pm — and they never allowed any lateness. I said to Mother I felt we couldn't go because we could not arrive late, and I knew that we could not arrive on time. I was feeling very nervous because I was sure we'd be turned away and would create such a bad impression.

Mother said: "Don't worry. Harold Vigurs is here in the car with us." I said, "What on earth is he doing here? I can't see him." Harold, I should explain, was a veteran Spiritualist. I couldn't even feel him, but believed my mother and said, "Well, if he is here — and I do believe you mother — tell him to go ahead and tell Silver Birch we are on our way and will arrive."

We went on. I kept saying to mother, "Now, you are sure?" because it was unheard of to arrive late at these meetings. We arrived...half an hour late. As I was about to ring the bell, the door opened and Barbie said: "Oh there you are! I was just going to look to see if you had arrived." I apologised. Barbie said he had realised it was foggy and that we might be delayed. I accepted this with relief.

In those circles, we always sat with the table before Silver Birch spoke so that various friends, relatives and other guides could be greeted. Well we, Mother and I, asked if my father was there, but no, he wasn't. Nor were any of our friends that we might expect. But Harold Vigurs was!

When it came time for Silver Birch to speak, he opened with the most beautiful prayer and then spoke to us, each in turn. When he came to me he said: "I received your message! Mr Vigurs came to me and told me you were held up." I turned to every one and told them what had happened. I was amazed, but my mother just smiled as if to say, "I told you so!"

This shows, doesn't it, that Barbie, who assumed he was waiting because of the fog, did not know that Silver Birch had received the message from Mr Vigurs and was influencing him to wait. He wouldn't have waited normally because he was meticulous about starting on time. Barbie wasn't clairvoyant himself so Silver Birch couldn't have just passed on the message in that way, but he was able to exert some influence on Barbie's mind.

Over the years, the evidence has piled up so much, but it does seem to be so much better through trance mediums.

Chapter 6

GOING TO WAR

WAR itself is a terrible thing. The wanton destruction of life and dreams cannot be rationalised or excused and yet here we were, faced with a terrible dilemma. The excess and wickedness of Hitler was not truly recognised until later on, but the knowledge that his ambitions and dreams meant the end of freedom for many others was only too apparent to us when war was declared. Sometimes even Spiritualists must take up arms to defend mankind from evil.

I shouldn't have gone into the army before I was 21, but I went before my age group and so had my 21st birthday in the Forces. At first, I dreaded the months in front of me, for that was the length of time I had expected to stay in the army, but later I came truly to believe that it was a necessary experience for me. As a gifted medium, I was able to help so many young men who were troubled.

So many I knew would pass. These I could talk to about the continuation of life and the reality of the spirit world. Of course, I could not reveal my knowledge of their destiny, but I was, in some way, able to prepare the ground so that their passing was not such a frightening experience. Many have since returned to me to thank me for the help I was able to give them at that time.

There were others who needed my knowledge to use in their future life here on earth and even, at times, the comfort of my presence near them for I knew that I would survive the war.

This gave me great confidence, which was infectious. I am still in contact with some of those whom I met and became friendly with during those years. There is a great bonding force between people who share a common danger.

I believe I was intended to go into the Forces. I fought like other people, but on my identity disk I insisted that I had my own religion inscribed, not Church of England or Baptist but Spiritualist so that if I was to be taken during that time I would go from this world named as a Spiritualist and proud to be one.

When I first went into the army in Bodmin, Cornwall, I explained that I was Spiritualist — and was smartly informed there was no such religion! Other well-known Spiritualists had the same difficulty. I was taken before the Commanding Officer for refusing to accept the word "Spiritist" other than the full title, Spiritualist. Eventually, I am proud to say that they agreed — and I was "tagged" with my correct description.

The Spiritualists' National Union tried to have ministers appointed to serve members in the Forces, but they were not successful in this. They did appoint ministers during those years to enable them to travel more freely in restricted areas, but we were too few to influence the army overmuch.

I made no secret of what I was or the special religion which was my strength. Although I was so young, I had a great deal of confidence for I had already been working as a medium for eight years and built a good reputation in that time. Having been brought up to mix with older people — many of whom had a great deal of knowledge — I was able to talk about Spiritualism as well as being able to prove my point through my mediumship.

I made many friends whom I knew were going to survive the war because a medium is conscious not only of the past and present, but also the future as well. When mediums are working, they are not conscious of time, but are sharing a consciousness of no time. We are conscious of an existence that goes beyond the present.

It was when I began to experience this I found I was able to talk to people. I was aware they were fearing death and could share the experiences I had had. Sometimes I was able to give them contact from the spirit world with family who had already passed over which helped them to know that there was life and hope and even laughter beyond the barriers of death.

Sometimes I could tell them about things that would happen in their future life and they had faith in me. Then I knew why I had to go into the army. I had thought I would hate every minute of it, but it was not so. I found I began to love every minute of it. I met so many people and was able to help many of them.

I started to hold circles, at first with one or two, but eventually sometimes having as many as forty or fifty of these young men all wanting to know more about life after death. These were the first steps to helping many young men who had been torn from their families to go to war and, perhaps, never to return.

I had so many wonderful experiences in those years and knew that Spirit were taking care of me. My men also started to realise this so they liked to be near me when there was enemy fire.

It must have been difficult for some of them to understand just how closely I was aware of the world of spirit. Often I knew that a companion was to pass quite soon. Sometimes I was able to see someone from his family with him and could tell him about this. Because I was right, he would listen: because he could recognise what I was saying as truth, he would have thoughts about the meaning of life. I am convinced this helped at the time of their passing. It is good to have had these thoughts for it brings the world of spirit near to even those who do not see or hear.

One time we became trapped behind the enemy lines. Our escape route, a bridge, had been blown up. There seemed to be no way out; there was a river, but we knew it was treacherous and very deep in places.

I had been taught how to swim in full kit, but not everyone could do so. I was in charge and wondered what I could do to save these men and get back to our lines. There is a point where sheer panic sets in when you think about what might happen. Everyone was looking to me for a solution.

I went aside and spoke with my spirit friends, saying: "You know the situation. We need to cross, but don't know the safe places." Desperately I asked for help. Cuckoo was there, and said I was to trust her. She promised to show me the way, and said, "Remember the bouncing ball!" Cuckoo reminded me of the first game we used to play together; now she would use that to bring us all to safety.

Approaching the water, I saw the ball. I knew that I must follow and I must trust. We crossed that river with the water sometimes up to our chins. We all got through, even those who were shorter than the others. The water did not come up higher than our chins.

To this day, I do not know how it happened, but I know that it did! How pleased we were to be safe on the right side of that river. It is little wonder that the platoon loved my little Black guide. Some of them collected pictures of Black children and named them Cuckoo. They had come to trust and to love my little friend.

Later, I was with the British Expeditionary Forces evacuated at Dunkirk, then went to Algiers through to Tunisia and Cape Bonne. We then went over to Sicily and through Italy. I was recommended to become an officer, but by that time my platoon were all friends and I didn't want to leave them.

I lost some friends in the evacuation of Dunkirk. There was such confusion on the beaches there. Enemy aircraft kept flying over, shooting at us and at our only form of transport, a positive armada of ships and boats waiting to evacuate us to England and safety. Men were sitting, standing, lying, moving, dodging the machine-gun fire from the enemy. The noise and heat were unbelievable. We were afraid, of course, but the incredible courage of the men and women on those beaches was a light in the darkness of despair. We could not give way to our baser emotions, but had to carry on.

I was waiting for instructions to board, but was suddenly overcome with a terrible thirst. I felt I just had to have water and went off in search of a tap. When I returned, I could not find my companions. I searched all over, but could not see them.

In the end, I gave up and was told to take a place on a ship. As soon as I boarded I felt so very sleepy. I found a space on the deck and lay down. In the midst of all that noise and movement I went into a deep, deep sleep. I did not awake until we reached England. When I did, those who were near to me told me what had happened as I slept.

An aeroplane had passed overhead intent upon strafing the decks of our ship. The pilot was on a direct path over where I lay, but his guns failed to fire. The plane went over me, then down and crashed into the sea. I had known nothing of this as I lay unconscious, but I realised that my life had been spared together with that of those near me. When I joined up with my platoon, I found several missing. The ship upon which I was supposed to embark had been machine gunned and hit.

I had known I would not die in the war; I had work to do for Spirit — and they had the plans well laid. I would live on! It was necessary for the prophecy to be fulfilled, but it was with great humility that I recognised this fact yet again. I did not in truth believe that this incident had just been coincidence, but saw in it the wonder of spirit intervention. My birth had been foretold; Spirit had told my mother about my future responsibilities. I had been specially trained in a family who had accepted the task. I had a destiny which could not be denied.

Later on I went to Greece and there, on one of the mountains on observation duty, I met with great friendship. An old lady very kindly brought me coffee and food. We were not able to talk because I did not speak her language and she spoke no English, but she came back many times to give me this comfort. It was particularly welcome because our rations were rather spartan. I thought from the first that she was a very great lady. Although we could not communicate, we seemed to understand each other and to see spirit in each other.

When we moved on to Athens, I met a very beautiful young lady. She was a superb pianist and I got to know her very well. I moved from the tent we had into a room in her house. A great friendship grew between us. We used to go to concerts and recitals together. Being involved herself, she was able to get tickets when others could not. One day we were talking about Spiritualism and she said she knew a very elderly lady who was like me and had the same experiences.

I was naturally very interested and told my friend so. The time came when she arranged for me to meet this person. We went into the mountains...and I suddenly realised that I recognised where I was going. We arrived at a little shack — and there was my old friend who had brought me coffee and bread. I threw my arms around her because I loved her, and explained to the others what had happened.

We sat in circle with her and before long had the most wonderful phenomena with spirit forms so solid we could touch them. They were the most marvellous materialisations I have ever experienced. I asked later through my interpreter how she had first known I was on the mountain for I was hidden from view. The old lady told me she had heard a voice telling her of my position and that she was to take me food.

I realised just how wonderful Spirit really is to have arranged this meeting of spirits when there was so much other work that they had to do. I had come to the conclusion that because of my special gifts I was used very much by Spirit in my sleep state to help in places where my body could not go. I have since spoken to other mediums who went through the war and found they are also of this opinion.

It was a great comfort to me because I was necessarily involved in the taking of life. I suffered mentally. I think thousands were in the same dilemma, but we had little choice. Our lives were directed for us during those tragic years. We cannot avoid the fact that all we do that is against the spiritual law must be recompensed. I was provided with the opportunity to give a little in return for all that I had received and to help the spirit world — and for that I am grateful.

A great friend of mine, I will call him George, was very interested in Spiritualism so we often talked together. His father had passed away before he came into the war. He loved his father dearly and still missed him.

One day in one of the battles in Italy I became aware of the presence of my friend. I realised he was dead, but that he was not aware of this. George lay by my side as I was watching the bombs falling onto their target.

"I thought that I had got it that time," he said. "Then I remembered you said that you would come out of the war safely, that there was no bullet with your name on it." I started to speak to George, but one of the sergeants thought I was speaking to him. At first I didn't like to tell the sergeant I was speaking to the spirit of someone both he and I knew, but eventually I had to.

The sergeant did not really understand. "How can you know George is dead?" he asked. "No one knows who is alive or dead yet." Well, of course, I did because George was there.

I spoke to him, saying: "George, your father loves you very

much. He can do far more for you now than I can. If you look ahead, you see him. You must go towards him and he will guide you." Naturally, his father came and took my friend with him into his next life. I watched them go together and felt very happy for them.

This incident strengthened my own understanding and also helped many to speak to me about life and death. So many of those who passed have come back to me over the years. They are truly not lost, but merely "gone before." I often think about them upon Armistice Day and how different this day is for us who know the truth.

It is hard now to think of all the young men and women who passed into the world of spirit during those years. We, who are Spiritualists, have much to be thankful for. We grieved when it was one whom we had become close to on this earth, but knew, you see. We did not have to just believe in life after death: we knew that it was really true. We are born to go through this life, not to stay for ever. When our time is come, we go on into our reality and this life is as a dream.

Naturally, in all sorts of conditions and situations the inner self, the soul, is linked up with the God figure of our universe. Within us all is this great power, this great light, which governs all. As my friends were killed during the war, many returned to me and have done in the years since then.

Spiritualism gives meaning: it shows you that you are not here by mistake, but that there is a purpose behind your presence in this life; that there is a Divine Law. It is this sort of thing that keeps us going, the knowledge that life is not just three score years and ten, but is continuous. There are many changes to life, many changes yet for us to meet and experience.

How nice it is to know that life goes on endlessly. We are not told how it goes on since we are not ready yet to be able to accept some of the divine and wonderful things that happen in our life. Only when we are ready can we move forward and see other things.

The trouble with our world is that people have closed down upon the truth. They think life is just as it appears, but there is so much more.

So many have come back to me to tell of how if only they had known the truth, how differently they would have lived their lives because they would have found a purpose that only death brought to them. We should know this before we pass so we can take up the threads which continue into the other life we will live in when we move into the spirit world.

Chapter 7

TRAINING FOR LIFE

BECAUSE so many young men had gone virtually straight into the war and did not receive the training that was required to earn a good living, a number of courses were offered.

I started on one of these before I left Greece. Called OCTU courses, they were designed to give the men added skills for when we were demobbed. This particular course was in window dressing, much concerned with the use of colour.

I had always been interested in colour through my mediumship and still find the use of it in my work very exciting. Here I was in a country which had been ravaged by war and learning about things which would be of use to me in all aspects of my future life. In spite of the conditions, I took so much of value from that country! I was very good at courses and did extremely well on this one. I was thoroughly enjoying my life at this time.

I had made very good friends in Greece and was able to indulge my taste for the arts as well as appreciating the beauty of the country. I was even allowed to take over the front window of the biggest store in Athens and design the display from start to finish. The papers made quite a lot of this and took pictures of it, but I did not have a copy. I do regret not having had a picture of the final design. I had used shoes of different colours and had ribbons streaming down from each shoe. I do still have my memories. Perhaps they are the best memento in the end.

I then went on a course of sales management, display and publicity which helped when I came out of the army and went to Technical College. I cannot really remember much of my feelings when I came home except that I knew that I wanted to change. I was in the forces for six and a half years because I was called up too early and then got caught up in the war.

I never regretted the experience. I remember the comradeship, the friends, many of whom I am still in touch with, the places where I held circles, always helping the spirit world to do their work. It is important to a medium to be able to empathise with many conditions and different experiences. It makes it so much easier for Spirit to pass on their feelings if the medium has some knowledge of the feeling being conveyed.

Even when I came out of the Forces I was made aware that Spirit were taking an interest in what I did. I didn't want to go back to the firm where I had been working. I liked the work and had taken advantage of the opportunity offered to those who were due to be demobbed of taking a training course. I chose to take management and window dressing. We were supposed to tell the firm where we had been working before we were called up that we were available again. I didn't!

I felt that so much had happened. I was a different person. I didn't want to go back. Rather, I wanted to seek new opportunities. It was a peculiar feeling to be in a normal environment again. In some ways I had lost six and a half years of my life, but in others I had gained far more than six and a half years of experience. Now I felt that to go back to my old job would just be starting up again where I had been all that time ago. As far as they were concerned, I was still the twenty-year-old who had limited experience. That was not the way I viewed myself.

I said to my mother I would go for sittings for advice. I travelled south to London where I knew of a number of excellent mediums of good repute who didn't know me. I wanted to be sure of which direction to take. I had some very good sittings with Annie Brittain, Billy Redmond, Ena Twigg and Joe Benjamin. Though I received some very good survival evidence, none of them gave me any idea of what I should do for the future, which was what I really wanted.

I went home. My mother said to me, "You're disappointed." I admitted I was so she offered to give me a sitting. I had a great respect for mother's mediumship, but she wanted things for me that I did not think were right at that time. I agreed, but only if she gave me a trance sitting. I didn't want her to know what she was telling me. Neither did I want her to be influenced by what she was feeling or hearing. I said to her that she would tell me what she wanted for me if she could hear what was being said.

I think it was at this point in my life that I realised the true value of the trance condition for in trance she would not be influenced by her own feelings. My mother understood and wasn't cross that I said these things for she understood how mediumship works and knew I was right. She agreed, and we sat together.

I was given such excellent evidence about a ring which had been given to me by a lady during the war years. This lady had made me promise always to wear this as it had been a special ring for her and she wanted me to have it. I had agreed that I would. I was very fond of her and appreciated this gift.

I had been sent up to Scotland to be trained with others to swim across lakes with all my kit on, even my boots. It was part of the training for the second front in the war. One day I realised that my ring had come off while I was in the water. My finger must have shrunk with the cold. Being numb, I had not even felt the ring come off. I was very upset, but could do nothing about it.

Well, this lady came back through my mother, who knew nothing at all about this, telling me she knew what had happened and was not cross that I had not kept my promise for she understood. She went on to say she had a duplicate of the ring in Spirit and would keep it for me for when I went over. The lady repeated all the details of my loss. This proved to me that my mother was in trance because of the way it was coming.

The guide then told me that my future lay in a certain direction. I didn't want to go in this direction and said so. "You will have three letters," he added. "I want you to promise you will open the first one you receive and accept what is in it."

Well, I waited. I had written for three jobs, one being in London where I wanted to go because I had a friend down there. The other two were in the Midlands, one in Stafford. If I could not have the London position, then I wanted the Stafford job because it looked to be interesting work with opportunity for advancement.

When the letters arrived, there were only two. I opened the one with the Stafford stamp. It was from my old firm who had heard that I was back. They were in Wolverhampton, but the postmark was from Stafford. Within a quarter of an hour the postman came back and apologised. He had the third letter in his hand; it had been misplaced and not delivered with the other two. It was the very letter I had wanted and would have opened first had I received it with the other two. I had made my promise to Spirit and knew I should have to keep it and so went back to my old firm.

My mother had said my destiny lay there and was quite right. I would not believe her and I argued with Spirit when they said that it was so. If I had seen the Wolverhampton postmark and had not opened that letter first, I would not have achieved the things I did eventually. In any other position, I could not have done the things I have been able to if I had not kept my promise to the spirit guide who advised me through my mother that day.

This made me determined that trance mediumship was the way I wanted to develop. I thought that if ever someone wanted a sitting and I knew them too well not to be influenced, I would be able to give a trance sitting and know nothing about it. The close contact with Spirit is so enhanced through the trance work.

Anyway, when I came out of the Forces I resumed my spiritual work. I hadn't ever really stopped working even during the war because Spirit will use the medium no matter what the surrounding circumstances. A lot of churches lost congregations during the war. So many young people were called up: many women had to take jobs so that the country could continue. Longton church was in a similar situation.

They asked my mother to take the Thursday and Saturday service so they could earn some money to keep the doors open. The Sunday congregation had dropped to almost nil during the war because of the circumstances.

I was naturally very concerned and went along to the Annual General Meeting since I had it in my mind that a friend of mine and a very good worker, Norman Tabbinor, would be president. I didn't want the position really. I had been the vice-president when I was 18 before the war, and didn't really want to take on an official position. I did not wish to be tied down particularly. The spirit world, however, decreed that I would be asked to take the president's job.

At the right time, I nominated Norman. Then someone

nominated me and another person seconded this. And before I knew where I was, I was the president of Longton! I thought it would be all right: I would work to see the church successful again and then go on my way, as it were. As with the army, I thought it wouldn't be for very long. I was wrong on both counts! I am still the president of the church all these years later.

The members gave me permission to choose my own committee. Norman became secretary. We knew it would be quite hard to rebuild the stability of the church, but determined to work as a team. I realised it would be best if we could own our own premises and decided to buy the church. We booked good mediums and advertised well.

The Spiritualists' National Union helped us with buying the church through its Building Fund Pool. We worked very hard, but could not have managed without the money we borrowed. Although I was always linked with the union through church affiliation, I had not really had time to think about my membership because I was busy developing and working as a medium before the war. I think that the loan they advanced made me think more about the union than anything else up to that time.

Over the years we have spent literally thousands of pounds on the church. This is how I understand the difficulties of our other churches so well because I had to go through the same difficulties at Longton. I know how hard it is to keep a church together in hard times. I have been very lucky at Longton because I've always had good people to help. The members of our church have always been loyal and supportive. I feel for the committees of churches who cannot find enough workers to help, who struggle to make ends meet and who give so much with such little reward.

And so in 1947 I became president of my church and have held that office ever since. It seems as if some of us are born to play out a spiritual role in this life as well as a material one and have to learn to blend the two. I do not regret all the time I have given to Spirit for I have been privileged to help thousands of people over the years and sometimes helped change their lives for the best. That gives me a very warm feeling. It is a tremendous lift in one's life to link with the spirit world and to work with them to help somebody who would not otherwise be able to cope with their problems.

I began my circle of development again to keep my mediumship going, and because I realised this would strengthen it. In this I followed all that my mother had taught me, and eventually started my physical circle. Even today I am close to people who sat in this circle those many years ago. We have scripts of those meetings recording the wonderful instances of both physical and spiritual phenomena, phenomena that proved without doubt the continuity of life.

I remember in one of the seances a woman had been invited whose husband had passed away. She was unknown to any of us. Her husband materialised and walked towards her, telling her his name and of his undying love. He told her of things that she had done since his passing and her actions at the cemetery.

It transpired the husband had watched as she refused to have earth scattered directly upon his coffin, but had ivy leaves cover the coffin. The earth after it was used to fill the grave. As he approached her in the seance, he asked her to hold out her hand and in it placed an ivy leaf. It was not until afterwards when she had recovered from her natural emotion that she was able to explain to us the significance of the ivy leaf.

The wife had taken the leaves to the cemetery from her garden — and identified the leaves that had been apported into the circle at the end of the seance as the very same variety. We had so many wonderful instances that other religions might term miracles, but that we in Spiritualism recognise as the power of our spirit friends who are able to manifest in, and have effect upon, our physical world.

These things change peoples' lives; they discover that there truly is life after this life, and that there is a God, a tremendous creative power. It seems that this God gives part of itself. It is as a tremendous, flowing power that seems to be awakened by a law.

I suppose we would call this a natural and spiritual law. The two seem to go together. It is because of this that we, in Spiritualism, who have been born with these gifts are playing a tremendous part in helping this power continue its work of creating, of moulding, of expanding, of expressing itself; all these things that we seem to need at this present time.

How many 14-year-olds could have taken notice of the prophetic words of a medium as my mother did? Even being given the proof, as she was, of her mother's return before she even knew that she had passed, how many would have kept faith with the prophesy? People say that you die and that is the end. How can this be when such wonderful things happen? That experience brought me into this world. Would I have been born at that time if it was not into that family which had been preparing for my advent for so many years?

Everything that has occurred, even to the medium giving me my spirit name, has happened to further my belief so that I would have the strength to do the work which it was intended for me to do. I believe that the friendships I have made have helped me along the way; I believe that Spirit has moved. But I am not alone, although the experiences of my life are extraordinary.

I have always believed that Spirit designs and patterns this world, and that within all of us is some purpose, a mission in life. The problem with most is that we have failed to look for it and also failed to have faith in something beyond our own self.

Not everyone will have a great mission, although who are we to question and decide which is great and which is less? We with the Gifts of the Spirit have a greater responsibility. It may be that it will be our task to bring that enlightenment to another human soul, enabling them to see clearly which is their pathway, where lies their strength and what is their mission.

Chapter 8

POST WAR YEARS

ALTHOUGH I had again become so involved with my church I did not see my future limited to one centre, especially in administration, I was — and still am — first and foremost a medium. I fully expect to end my days in harness and will thank God if I am allowed this privilege.

I resumed taking bookings, again in my own area, but this was soon to alter. Before I had been called up, I was termed "The boy wonder" by local papers. This was due, in no small measure, to the fact that my mother was so demanding in my training. I had learned to listen to Spirit and was able to give full names and addresses even then. I started to take larger meetings...and enjoyed them.

I found that my reputation had survived my absence. When I was advertised to take a meeting, the church or hall was always filled. Often many had to be turned away. I had started to get quite complicated messages which linked various people in the hall. This was of great interest to the papers and my reputation increased. I was still considered young. In those days, I was slim, with a good head of hair.

Although I was working locally, I was meeting some wonderful people. At Hebden Bridge Spiritualist Church, Jessie Green was the president. Jessie was the only female president of the Spiritualists' National Union, and the only one also to be president of the Lyceum Union as well as the SNU. She was a wonderful lady, was so kind and sent in a glowing report of my work to "Psychic News."

I was invited to take part in the Centenary Meeting at the Civic Hall, Wolverhampton in 1948. I was only booked for the afternoon, but Harold Vigurs asked particularly if I could stay on to work with him in the evening. This was a tremendous honour for me. I have to acknowledge the generosity of the medium who stood down to let me take his place.

There were over a thousand people — and I was nervous! I was also very aware of Mr Vigurs and the other well-known people who were there; they had so much knowledge and experience. I really felt young at the moment of walking out on to the platform. I bless my mother for her training and my guides for their loving support through all the years of my development. They were so close to me; I felt that I could reach out and touch them. This gave me the courage and confidence to begin.

As soon as I started working, the magic took over and I was aware only of Spirit. Afterwards, I remembered the applause and took pleasure in that thrill of knowing that I had justified the effort of those who had worked with me for so long and the trust of those who had invited me on to the platform to work with them at this important meeting. I couldn't wait to speak with my mother and family for I knew that they would be so pleased for me.

I have always enjoyed working for Spirit. Likewise, I do enjoy working on the public platform. I cannot understand those who say they do not, but that Spirit point them in this direction. How can others enjoy watching if you do not like giving?

Of course, it was not always straightforward. I recall one meeting at Moston, arranged by the church and the Lyceum. I worked quite a lot for the Lyceum for I had always been associated with them from when I was very young in Longton.

At this meeting I gave a gentleman the name of Harthill, but he had not recognised this. I had to accept that and went on. Later, I went to a lady. She recognised this name and was related to the first gentleman. Then I linked about three other people with the same message, getting more and more details.

In the end, the first man also recollected the communicator. All was well in the end, but it took some time and effort on behalf of the spirit people. I knew I was right, but didn't argue. I just worked on and left it to Spirit to sort out. And they did!

Having seen the way I worked and expressed his feeling that I should be invited to London, Harold Vigurs was a man of his word. He arranged for me to stay with him and to work at Croydon Spiritualist Church. It was such a change. Usually it was London mediums who were feted in the provinces. Here was I reversing the process. I found that Harold had spoken so well about my abilities that the church was packed to capacity and I received several other invitations.

The first meeting I took in Central London was wonderful. I was so nervous, but a success. Papers accused me of being theatrical sometimes, but they didn't know that this was sheer nervous tension. The Victoria Halls in Bloomsbury were famous and to work for the Marylebone Spiritualist Association — now the Spiritualist Association of Gt Britain — who had organised the meeting was, at that time, the sign that you had arrived. Most of the well-known mediums had been there. Here was I, a provincial, just making my mark on the great metropolis.

Running Water, the guide of much-loved healer Nan Mackenzie, gave a superb address which was a marvellous boost for me as well as for those assembled. It is always easier to work when the audience is attuned spiritually. No one listening to Running Water could have failed to achieve that state of mind. As usual, I gave names and addresses, even describing locations in order to prompt memories.

Afterwards a Mr and Mrs Hiscock, who had been given a message but not been able to accept all of the details, took the trouble to follow up the parts not recognised. They travelled the route which I described — and found I had been quite right. The couple passed a pub called the Plumbers Arms, realised that the shop, Spinks, was right there and then went on to find the shop with the name of Sean as described. It had been newly painted to show the name. Their neighbour was indeed named Emma, although they had not known this previously. It is not often people take the trouble to check on things that they cannot immediately recognise, but these two did and then wrote to "Psychic News" to give all the details.

It was while working in London that I became aware I must change my style to suit the different conditions. I had noticed that London mediums just called out the name of a communicator and waited for this to be picked up from the audience. This did not seem a particularly accurate or evidential way of working. I said so in an interview with "Psychic News."

I did, however, recognise the difficulties of finding a recipient in a hall where you could not easily see or point out the person you wished to speak to. I had a word with Helen Hughes, an experienced medium, fine worker and a wonderfully generous person. I sought her advice as Helen was able to go straight to her recipient. I asked her how she did this so quickly in a large hall. Helen said she had had the same problems and came to an agreement with her guide. In short, she would be shown a silver light over where she was to work.

I decided I must look at the way that I worked to find my answer. I realised that by going straight to my recipient, I was sometimes more aware of them and their needs than I was of Spirit. I must first become aware of Spirit, then I would ask for specific information which would identify the recipient. Odd Christian names thrown out at random would not do: I must give more accurate information. I did this. And it has paid off through the years. Of course, I can still get it wrong, but usually I am right, know this and I say so!

I had not been neglecting my church at Longton and worked there regularly. We had the debt to pay to the union and were determined to clear this as soon as we could. Thanks to the publicity given to my work, we were always sure of a full house when we put on special meetings. The papers said that 90 per cent of meetings were attended by women. So, in the late 1940s — I cannot recall the exact year — we devised a publicity gimmick to answer this charge.

We held a "Men only" week! This was remarkably successful. On the first night, a Saturday, we had to turn away over 100 as we were packed to capacity. Mr Hayward, on the platform with me, gave a fine address. He was the President of the Sheffield Psychic Research Society. During the meeting, I gave him a message from his father, which he accepted. Then he told us all that it confirmed a previous message when his father had stated he would communicate at Longton on November 7.

I often wonder how Spirit can be vague sometimes about time and then produce something like this that is so accurate and timed so well.

Our own male voice choir were there in force. We had fourteen members at that time and raised a good sum during the week towards our funds. Our ladies, not to be outshone, held their own meetings the following week. They, too, were well supported.

It was in the 1950s that I started to be really well known outside the Potteries and was given so many opportunities. I met Madam St Claire, a lovely lady who had lost her family during the occupation of France. She was a wonderful speaker on Spiritualism and the interpreter for me when I went with Harold Vigurs to Belgium for a series of meetings over there.

I was the first medium to work across the channel after the war. We received a marvellous reception. I was very thrilled because it was the first time I used an interpreter. In fact, in Brussels we needed two because it had to be translated into French and Flemish. Of course, I couldn't speak the language, but Spirit were so very close that I was able to work as usual, giving full names, although sometimes I had to spell them as I couldn't quite get my tongue around the accent. We went first to Liege.

It was very different from our type of meeting because there were no hymns, music or prayers. To one lady I brought back a relative, Raymond Biquet, and gave not one but two of his full addresses. This message was advice for the recipient's health. Another, from George Leon Minet, who was a director of insurance, was business advice for an old friend.

I worked for over two hours at that first meeting — and everything was understood and accepted. Even here, the communicators linked up people from other parts of the hall who were connected. I worked very hard, but it was good...and I was right!

Harold and I went on to Ghent and Bruge. It was a fantastic experience in many ways. I was a celebrity, which I did enjoy, but to see all the devastation and misery caused by the war counteracted that. I was able to bring help and comfort to many, many people during this visit and know that I expanded my own awareness of the ways in which Spirit can work. There is no language barrier.

I was pleased to be back home. I have always been very fond of my home, and that has not changed over the years. Whenever possible, when I am working away I return at night. This very often involves driving through the night, but I prefer to do it this way.

By now, most of my meetings were being covered by reporters. Sometimes, in the beginning, they grumbled a little. They were used to being able to position themselves to one side near the front. Being able to cover everything from that place quite easily, they found difficulties when I was working. I remember the meeting after which they complained. Their complaint was, I think, a little tongue in cheek and intended to highlight the difference in the way that I worked compared to other mediums.

It was at the Victoria Hall, London, for the Marylebone Spiritualist Association. Such complex messages were being given, linking together recipients in different parts of hall often through a third person. It was quite thrilling for me because it was going so well, but the reporters found this a headache as they had to concentrate on first one, then another. They didn't know where I would go to next or even if the message was being continued through another recipient.

In May, I was invited to take the union's London District Council annual convention. I was the only medium to take this for five consecutive years, which was a tremendous compliment. There used to be such fascinating people there. I know that in 1951 there was Richard Boddington, Lord Dowding, John Stewart and Harold Vigurs. I made one link with Herbert, son of Charles Williams of Peckham. He was a good communicator and gave me his father's name and address along with his date of passing, where he was living when he went and so many other details. It was a long communication involving so many people present who had known him that everyone felt a part of it.

I did enjoy that meeting. Haylock Eyre, who was a fine elocutionist, recited Sir Edward Arnold's poem, "Death's Chief Surprise" whilst Douglas Hemmings, a baritone, sang "The Lord is My Light" and "If I Can Help Somebody." Mr E. E. Philips, President of the old London District Council chaired whilst Harold Vigurs appealed on behalf of the Spiritualists' National Union's Fund of Benevolence and the Cannock Sunshine Home. They had combined choirs — and the atmosphere was so wonderful!

Of course, I was still considered to be very young and new, although I had been working for years and was in my 30s. But I was getting a lot of media coverage, not all good, but most of it was complimentary. Even so, I was still flattered to work with mediums like Bertha Harris, Helen Hughes and Estelle Roberts, who were really big names in Spiritualism.

In 1950, Spiritualist churches across England celebrated the news that Walter Monslow, MP, had drawn first place in the ballot to introduce a Private Members Bill. He had promised our friend in Parliament, Tom Brooks, that he would support our Freedom Bill. This was the culmination of years of work and the effort of thousands of Spiritualists in the country to repeal the Witchcraft Act of 1735.

The Fraudulent Mediums Act was not actually passed until June 22, 1951 for it had to be heard again in Parliament, but this was the beginning of the end of the persecution of mediums. No longer would mediums like Helen Duncan be prosecuted, as she was in 1944, just for doing her work. No longer would our churches stand in danger of prosecution just for opening their doors and permitting mediums to work on their platform as had happened during the last war.

This drew my attention again to the Spiritualists' National Union. I had worked with some of their best mediums and was now a Class B member. As I have said, I was associated with the Spiritualists' National Union through my church membership and also through the Lyceum movement to which I belonged. I had every intention of applying earlier, but time passed and I was very busy. Although I knew that my life's work was to be in Spiritualism, I did not then know that it was to be so closely involved with the union. I joined after the war, I think in 1946.

Leading Spiritualist Dorothy Hudson, when she saw me at Coventry church, said that I should go in for my CSNU, the award the union gives to mediums of a required standard. Dorothy was on the District Council even then! She and Jo Capstack, the then vice-president of the SNU, signed my application form. I delayed applying for my CSNU because I was not a speaker at that time. I had been thoroughly trained as a demonstrator, but not as a speaker.

Most churches booked speakers and demonstrators separately at this time so that mediums could concentrate their energies on just one skill or the other. I was able to speak since I was used to being one of the staff in the army. I had been taught how to lecture and to teach, but had not trained in the art of giving an address. I had to learn all that later on. There is an art to giving an address. Although I had a sound knowledge of Spiritualism, I had not then mastered that art.

I never worked at district level, and was not really interested in administration as I had enough of that in my own church! We were very busy there because it had become so run down. We had to build it up again and earn the money to repay the capital we borrowed to buy it.

I don't think that I would ever have worked at national level if it had not been for Stansted Hall, the lovely Essex mansion which now belongs to the union.

I had given a sitting to Arthur Findlay — its then owner — not long before he died. Still one of Britain's most famous Spiritualists — and author of several masterly, classic books upon our subject — it was he who left the hall to the union. When I heard the union were going to have to sell the hall, which houses the Arthur Findlay College, I thought that I must try to do something about it. And if it had not been for that I might never have fulfilled my destiny.

Chapter 9

FORMS MATERIALISE

I WAS sitting in a circle in the 1950s, but it was for trance. The guides said they wanted to develop my physical mediumship because they thought it would be valuable. We actually started with sixty sitters because as soon as I announced this would be my purpose everybody wanted to be included. Rather than say "No" to anyone, I decided we would accept all of those who asked.

I felt quite confident that Spirit would make sure we ended up with the right people, the ones they wanted. The development of physical mediumship can take a long time and requires a great deal of patience. Those who wanted to be in the circle for the wrong reasons would soon drop away. I was sure this would be the way — and so it was. We ended up with about 25 people who were very good, and sat together for many years.

The development of this gift is a specialised task. I have spoken to a number of mediums who are presently developing and think that these days it is not being done in the way it should be. The medium must be able to prove the continuance of life. There must, of course, be a someone capable of physical phenomena to start with. And the development must continue beyond the movement of objects.

There has to be a dedication by all the people involved, not just the medium, but also the sitters. If individuals come and go, then Spirit cannot set up the conditions on their side so the phenomena can take place. It is important that those in charge know the necessities for the protection of the medium. A lot of energy is used during these seances, far more than in an ordinary circle. This has to be replaced afterwards.

More is taken from the medium than the sitters so they must have a sweet drink or something to eat afterwards. You should never eat a heavy meal before sitting because the energies are then being used to digest the food and cannot be available for the use of Spirit. Caution must be used in the seance room to be sure that it is clean. Helen Duncan once had a pin embedded into her body which had been caught up as the ectoplasm withdrew from around her.

I have experienced burns and injury when my seances had unexpected interruption so you see how important it is to know what you are doing before you embark on this type of development.

As I said, we ended up with twenty-five in the circle. We met in the church as I wanted it to be a church circle. Anyway, with those numbers it could not really be in my home and so it was held at Longton church. It was a circle that was bigger than normal because the usual number for a physical circle is about ten. These people sat with me — and I never lost a sitter after Spirit sorted out who were to stay. There was a wonderful sense of purpose and unity.

We sat for several years developing physical phenomena. And no one missed a meeting unless they were ill. People would come back from their holiday to make sure that the continuity was not broken. It was some seven years before we were getting good trumpet and apport phenomena; we nearly always had one sometimes two trumpets moving. We had spirit lights and the movement of objects quite early on, of course, but this is only a start and does not prove survival.

Then, about 1964, we started to get materialisation, but I did not give public demonstrations until around 1970. Of course, we allowed people to come into our circle, those who had special needs or sometimes folk who had worked hard for Spirit and wanted to be included to witness these wonders from the next world.

Our first full materialisation was the father of Mrs Lowe, who always sat nearly opposite me with her friend Mrs Howe. The spirit form came out from the cabinet, went across to his daughter and spoke quietly in her ear. Mrs Lowe told us afterwards that he had called her by a special name known only to him. She would not reveal what that name was because, she said, "There are other mediums here who I hope will one day give me the same evidence."

As he walked away from her she called, "Father, you have forgotten to put your braces up again!" That was further evidence because her father never put his braces up properly, but used to let them dangle — just as his spirit form was doing. You see, it is not enough to have phenomena: survival evidence must be given.

It was quite funny with this lady because her husband kept coming, but she had not had a happy time with him on earth and refused to acknowledge him. One day he brought with him what looked like a charred log of wood in his arms. Well, we wondered what it could be, but knowing she would never accept him did not like to ask.

This particular time, Mrs Lowe was touched by the way he came and the object he carried. She told us the story behind it. Her husband had a wooden leg and used to beat her and her children unmercifully; this was the reason she did not want to acknowledge him because she just could not forgive him for the unhappiness he caused. She might have accepted his cruelty to herself, but not to the children.

In his rages he would sometimes lock them out and they had to spend the whole night in the open; they would huddle in the outside toilet for shelter. One day, Mrs Lowe went into the house and, while he was sleeping, took his wooden leg and burned it. This was the log which he carried in his arms. Mr Lowe knew how wrong he had been, but his wife was never able to forgive him.

It was so rewarding to see the pleasure that these spirit contacts brought. I never saw it, but people would tell me afterwards. It made up for the fact that I could never see the wonderful things that happened. Their obvious pleasure in the evening made up for my missing it all.

Our circle became quite famous. Many mediums came to visit: Clara Shakespeare, Edith Guy, Mr and Mrs Woodhouse, Albert Taylor — all well-known demonstrators at that time. Healer Harry Edwards sat with us and many others. We made no charge. Often the mediums would stay over if they had come a long way. We didn't use cars quite so casually then so a lot of people relied upon public transport.

We started our seance with an invocation and then had one

short hymn. I would take that opportunity to go into trance. Once I was entranced, the proceedings were then handled by the spirit guides. Notes were always taken of what happened in the circles. Kath Jebb-Jones was meticulous in carrying out this task, and we were very grateful to her for doing this. It is important that all proceedings in circles should be noted for future reference.

When I became the vice-president of the union I had to give my circle up. There was just too much work to do. I decided that this commitment was too much. I still sat occasionally. Indeed, it was the circle guides who always gave me good advice when I had a problem.

Of course, two of my guides have become so well-known to people through my physical mediumship; they are Cuckoo and Paddy. Cuckoo, as already explained, has been with me ever since I can remember, a great friend to me over the years. Paddy usually takes charge during physical seances and is very good. I have another guide called Choo Chow of whom I was aware, but who did not come forward until the beginning of my trance mediumship and seemed to take charge. It was through him that I became a trance speaker. He is very much with me when I am teaching.

I have another guide who only comes to me once a year. He takes over during my regular Christmas Day trance address, speaking about the world and the current and future situations. He gives predictions about the twelve months ahead. The idea is that we are coming to the end of the year and meet at the church. It is nothing to do with the Christian festival, but the spirit people seem to feel that this time of the year is important to them as well as to us. They, too, meet together to discuss what help is needed.

This guide predicted the fall of the Berlin Wall: it is recorded where he said that the wall between the East and the West would disappear, mentioning upheavals in the world. He spoke of the coming resignation of Margaret Thatcher, that though she had done her part, it was time for other people to take over. This guide is Light. I am named after him in the spirit world.

There were some who sat with us who went on to become mediums themselves. Two such sitters were Victor and George Wood. They became physical mediums and were very good. They donated the window of the Good Shepherd in our church in memory of their mother and father who both returned in our circle over the years.

Kitty Jones moved away to Wales and is working. There were others, but generally the sitters were happy just to give their time and effort to further the work of Spirit through my mediumship. This is why there are so few good physical mediums now. The dedication needed is immense since the time it takes to develop can be years. Everybody wants everything at once these days: they don't want to wait.

I have to say that I often found it frustrating to hear about the trumpet moving or spirit materialising and knowing that all ceases before I came back into consciousness. I have seen all these things in other circles because I was able to sit with some marvellous physical mediums, such as Helen Duncan, Bill Olsen, Trevor Davis, Alec Harris and, of course, Jack Webber.

However, because people were getting so much spiritually this compensated for my not being able to witness the marvels that were going on. I also think that the help and guidance I have received over the years from the spirit world has been a very great repayment to me. I have been helped over such difficult patches in my life and couldn't have survived without the love and advice I have been given.

I would like to say here it is not the movement of objects that is important in physical mediumship, but the proof of survival that comes with this. I am completely against trumpets floating about and tables lifting without the evidence. People that are scientific know these things can be produced without the intervention of the spirit world.

With Olsen, his jacket came off even though it was sewn on to him, but you could always see the ectoplasm there. I had one experience with him when the trumpet fell right by my feet. I gripped it tightly between my feet to prevent its further movement and then felt a sort of plunger acting on my toe. I could feel the sucking of it. Then it went to the trumpet. Even though I pressed as hard as I could, I could not prevent the trumpet from being slipped out of my grip.

There was no question that Spirit had removed it. I did confess afterwards that I had been testing to see whether there was an intelligence behind the movements. But the trumpet didn't just wave around in random fashion; it would circle the sitters and stop in front of whoever was being spoken to before moving on.

I sat with Helen Duncan several times. At one seance a little bird materialised and also what looked just like a little fairy. I suppose you could call it a nature spirit. She held out her hands. The forms just sat there before eventually flying away. You don't think that fairies exist really, but when you see them you have to change your mind.

When I sat with another medium, Mrs Pope, the room became filled with butterflies. She had ping-pong balls covered with luminous paint. They used to bounce up and down. The butterflies settled on the curtains — and there was so much light you could see your face. Harold Vigurs was there...and we were fascinated.

One time I remember Brigadier Firebrace, from London's College of Psychic Studies, told me that Olsen had been with them the previous evening, and they had sat together with others. The chairs were all upon a large carpet.

During the seance, they received some marvellous evidence, but when the lights were put on at the end of this meeting they found that the carpet had been removed from under them and was folded neatly in the middle of the circle! With these mediums there was always verbal evidence as well. We have to be aware that there needs to be evidence of intelligent direction in any type of phenomena for them to be of real value.

In the late 60s, before the alterations to Stansted Hall, Gladys Mallaburn worked with me in the lounge. We sat behind a screen across the bay window, and both went into trance at the same time. About sixty people were able to see her guide and mine working, each doing their own work. She was at the height of her physical mediumship then. We also held a circle outside in the grounds of Stansted Hall together with friends. It was at midnight around: we sat around the Tulip tree where everyone saw spirit's forms build up.

We were — and still are — great friends, Gladys and I. She is a minister of the SNU and a good worker for the spirit world. When Gladys' husband died tragically, I gave her daughter away at her wedding. Her daughter was born a Spiritualist and was named in the Spiritualist church. In Spiritualism, the naming service indicates not just an acknowledgement of the soul's link with the spirit world, but also the acceptance of the child into our Spiritualist community. This naming service was undertaken by the spirit guide of Hunter Selkirk.

The spirit form materialised during the ceremony and actually held the child and did the naming ceremony. I have never heard of any other child who was held and named by a materialised form. That was in Newcastle-upon-Tyne; you don't get physical mediumship like that these days. Hunter Selkirk was a great medium for Spiritualism.

As I said, there is so much impatience now: people will not wait until marvellous things like these are possible. They are content just to see things moving about and won't wait for all the things we know are possible. It is a great pity. Of course, there have been many changes in the conditions from those years. There are so many different vibrations about these days not just from human beings, but from machines, videos and television. I do think this makes a difference. There are a few physical mediums now, but not of the calibre of those who could produce such wonderful proof of survival.

Let me repeat my belief that Spiritualism is not about the moving of trumpets; it is not about the tinkling of bells. It is about the communication of people who have lived upon the earth. When the body has died, human personality continues to exist. The mind not only continues to exist after death, but has added further experiences to the sum total of its knowledge. Physical mediumship is a natural gift which must be developed in a spiritual manner.

Chapter 10

SPIRIT PROMISE KEPT

THESE days people want everything with no effort. I have seen and heard of those who expect physical phenomena in a year or less! My circle sat for about seven years before we got trumpet and apport phenomena — and then it was even longer before we started to get full materialisation.

I did not give public demonstrations until about 1970. As I said before, we allowed people to come into our circle. It would have been easy to have guests every week, but that is not the purpose of a physical circle. When the guides say it is all right, then guests can come in. So many have never witnessed this type of phenomenon.

Early in 1970 my good friend and colleague, Frank Tams, built a cabinet for me to use in the library at Stansted Hall. The cabinet is not to conceal anything that is happening, but used to focus the energy around the medium for Spirit to utilise in their work. Although there are curtains, these are usually drawn back so people can see clearly what is happening.

Veteran Scottish Spiritualist Dr John Winning was present for one of the first of many demonstrations we held there. He described the ectoplasm emerging as "like fine strands of wool about nine inches thick at floor level." Forms built, but were unable to emerge from the cabinet. However, Dr Winning recognised the voices of two old friends, Will Edwards and a man named Suttleworth. He had heard both so many times at Lyceum conferences that he declared he could not mistake their tones.

Later that year we had a far more successful session. Eileen Roberts, currently president of the Institute of Spiritualist Mediums, sat on one side of me with Dr Winning upon the other.

All these who cry "Fraud!" do not know the worth of those who sit with me. The integrity of these two who held my hands, who reached out and felt all the varying textures of the ectoplasm change within seconds, and who have vouched for my work, is above reproach.

Those who were invited to help most intimately with these seances were chosen especially. Not for their friendship for me, not for their desire to share the glory for that was most certainly not necessary for them, but rather for their knowledge, for their intelligent understanding of what happens during the manifestation of physical phenomena.

At this seance a full form, the daughter of one sitter, walked from the cabinet to a distance of about two feet. She was fully materialised above her knees and gave the most wonderful evidence of her identity. Medium Robin Stevens, now International Spiritualist Federation president, was there. He received an apport, a torpedo-shaped capsule, which he identified as being the form of medication taken by his communicator prior to his passing into the spirit world.

The results were getting better. In June, we had a good materialisation where medium Ruth Lewis was present. She was thrilled, having been promised over twenty years ago that she would one day see Spirit in this way. I think she had just about given up hoping. Cuckoo, who was sitting upon my knee, took Ruth's hand. She felt the pulsation of the living ectoplasm. Apparently, another form which built beside us could be seen quite clearly. I was still visible, sitting quietly towards the front of the cabinet.

I am not surprised that people flock in the hope of seeing physical phenomena. I have been lucky that I was able to sit with other mediums and so witnessed the marvellous power of the spirit world. It is vital that the medium should have built up a trust and rapport with spirit helpers over their development. I have been injured through the carelessness of someone who was permitted into a group seance at Stansted Hall, and who used a tape recorder without permission.

Spirit will often allow electrical apparatus, cameras and even limited light to be used during the manifestation of the phenomena, but always with permission. Although I have studied this type of mediumship, even I do not always understand why just a little deviation can have drastic effect. I know that it can so always took as many precautions as possible.

I well remember the time in question. I had been very interested in expanding our knowledge of physical mediumship and started some experiments at Stansted Hall using infra-red filming techniques.

John Hughes, a professional photographer from London, and M. H. Tester, the well-known healer and photography expert, participated in these sessions. Now I wanted to see if the physical phenomena could manifest without the use of a cabinet. I knew that this had been done in the past, although not very often. I wanted to see if it would work again. More than that, I wanted to go one step further. I believe that this is the way we learn, by always being prepared to go one step further.

Sometimes we are surprised by the results, but I don't think that Spirit ever are. They are usually willing to help us understand more. I needed to sit with people who had experience and thought of Hannen Swaffer's home circle which was held at Maurice Barbanell's flat in St John's Wood, NW London. Barbie was always a good friend to me and to the union. I trusted him, had visited this circle previously and knew it was right. He had some very good people helping him. The power in the lounge had built up over the years.

The seances at Stansted Hall had been very good, of course, but they could have been much better. The trouble was not just blacking out the library, but also the lack of people used to sitting together on a regular basis. Spirit build up not only power when they are working with a regular circle, but also a rapport. This was missing from the Stansted experiments.

Anyway, I agreed to hold a sitting at Barbie's flat. Apart from the wonderful spirit-filled atmosphere, I knew his sitters would also add to this, making conditions very favourable for the experiment I wanted to try.

I thought we could perhaps not use the small cabinet which was usual in physical seances. There was a small adjoining room which could be used to collect, store and hopefully focus the power. When we gathered, I was a little concerned because there was even more light showing than at Stansted Hall. This was one of the things that Barbie criticised about our seance there.

We still used a red bulb with a rheostat because we wanted to be sure that everyone would be able to see what was going on. Not knowing just how long the seance would last, we could not be sure of continued natural light.

I confess to being nervous. I always am just before I work. I do like things to go well — and this was the first time I had ever tried materialisation without the cabinet. I know it has been done occasionally by others, but not very often. This was the first time for me.

Well, of course, I can't tell just what happened because once I have induced my trance condition the guides take over. Peter Green from "Psychic News" was present. Peter, who later became a reporter for "Hansard," the Parliamentary journal, wrote describing the seance so I can recount from that just how well it went.

I was searched before the seance as a matter of record more than the possibility of having concealed anything. I never wear much more than trousers and a thin shirt with slippers during these events. Apart from the obvious check against the accusation of having material concealed about my person, there is also the question of heat. A lot of energy is used during physical mediumship. Most of it is concentrated around the medium.

John Hughes and M.H.Tester were to be there to take photographs if and when they were given permission from the spirit people. We met at Barbie's flat on March 7, 1975. After Charles Birkett, a Spiritualist for many, many years and member of the Silver Birch circle, had searched me we gathered into a circle.

I always insist that I am searched, even when the sitting is private because there are always people ready to cry fraud when they read about physical phenomena. I have never charged for these sittings because I have not felt it right to do so, though I've been offered huge sums of money if I would give sittings like these. Indeed, once I was offered £1,000 just for one evening. I can't say I have not been tempted, but I have still never charged.

Charles Birkett confirmed that I had nothing more on than was apparent and we sat down in a circle. Sylvia Barbanell took one of my hands, Barbie the other. We sat in the dining area whilst the regular sitters were just through an arch leading into the larger room. We were in full view at all times.

The guide greeted the circle and assured us that friends were already gathering on his side. Then Paddy took over; he is usually my chief communicator, although Cuckoo is always there. That seems to be Paddy's function. I will not go through the whole seance because it lasted quite some time and so many things happened, but I would like to recount one very moving part of the meeting.

Charles Birkett was overjoyed to be given an apported rose depicting both the name and the favourite flower of his late wife. He was even more delighted when she spoke gently to him and then, with tremendous effort, the ectoplasm flowing from my nostrils at that time, Rose struggled to assume the life form she had when on earth and was able to take on a solidity which was actually felt by Sylvia. Charles was not beside me and even though the form was unable to move far from me, he accepted her identity absolutely.

After this emotional experience, Paddy reduced the tension by announcing that the ectoplasm would now be taken from my solar plexus. At this the ectoplasm dropped away, leaving my face completely clear and, instead, streamed from my solar plexus. This move was not gradual, but an immediate falling away from my face to my body.

Another form materialised. Barbie could feel the softness of the surface layer of ectoplasm covering the solidity of the form beneath. The form could be felt quite easily about nine inches in front of and slightly above my own head. Remember, I was not in a cabinet, but still sitting openly in the circle. Some very good pictures were taken and reproduced in "Psychic News." As always happens, not everyone believed in the truth of what could plainly be seen.

This was a time when I was doing quite a lot of physical work, but I was never as good as I could have been. Although my circle sat for so many years, I was never able to give the time and attention to physical mediumship that I should have needed to get the best results.

I felt very strongly that as many people as possible should have the chance to witness phenomena. Most physical mediums choose to work in small groups. This is the best condition for phenomena, but my guides agreed that we should try to work in larger halls.

Dr Winning was a great support to me in this ambition. At the Glasgow Association of Spiritualists, I worked in a partially lit hall using a portable cabinet on the platform. Between two and three hundred people witnessed the phenomena.

First to materialise was a Mrs McConnell, mother-in-law to James McNee, who is also in Spirit. She gave so many intimate details, which delighted her two daughters and her grandchildren who were present. Dr Winning said that if the hall was properly blacked out the results would have been better, but could we have completely blacked out a room holding several hundred people in safety? Was it not better that so many could have the opportunity to say, "I have seen"?

That same year at the Spiritualists' Summer School I held an afternoon seance with about one hundred and thirty present. Full form materialisation took place. We had some good Summer Schools there in Wales. Eric Hatton, at present vice-president of the Spiritualists' National Union, was called "The Headmaster" and organised a superb team of lecturers and demonstrators. Eric, a minister and president of his local church, is usually so serious, but he has a wonderful sense of the ridiculous which you would never suspect.

I remember that Richard Ellidge, former general secretary of the union, stood in for Harold Vigurs. A good friend to me, Harold's passing was a sad blow for the movement. Olive Burton, who for many years worked with Harry Edwards, came down to do the healing talks. Pioneer Spiritualist Percy Wilson also worked hard. Another veteran, Mabel Hibbs, did the organising, and we had such a nice week. I have some wonderful memories to look back upon.

In 1974 I held another seance at Stansted Hall, which was very successful. It had been arranged for a German film company and was one in a series of four held over two days. We had some very good photos taken by John Hughes and M.H.Tester, using infra-red equipment.

At the time I was very eager to improve my faculties for physical mediumship and thought there was so much room for experimentation which had been neglected in recent years. The week in question was "Physical Phenomena Week" at the hall so it seemed very appropriate. We decided this would be right.

It was in November. As usual the room was thoroughly cleaned before being locked prior to the seance. Ronald Baker sat on my left. He was general secretary of the SNU at that time, and a very good medium himself.

Another well-known medium, Betty Wakeling from Blackpool, Lancs, was on my right. Tony Ortzen — he later edited "Psychic News" for ten years following Barbie's passing — searched the room and myself before we started and sat about six feet from cabinet. It is from Tony's report that I can recount what happened that evening.

The seance began with Oriental guides greeting from outside the cabinet. Paddy gave superb clairvoyant evidence of one sitter's daughter called Gill, who died in an avalanche in Austria. Gill materialised and stood outside the cabinet with me. It is not often that I move during a seance, but this time must have been an exception. Gill sent her love to her sister called Logie and her husband, David.

Gill mentioned her mother's "two little ones." Mrs Gains explained that these were dogs, often jokingly called "her children." Her married name was given and the initials BAC and BAG. Mrs Gains had been married twice. Her first initials, BAC, had changed to BAG. Gill spoke twice, once mentioning the orchid her mother had pressed from her wedding bouquet. This was a long communication, with many personal details given.

After this long seance I had to rest for a while, but was due to give a lecture in London at the Spiritualist Association of Great Britain at 7 pm. I drove there and arrived just in time. I finished that and then drove home to Longton. I remember that I was very tired!

Sometimes when wretched journalists or magicians say that these phenomena can be produced by trickery I get so cross. First why should we bother to set up such an elaborate hoax? Certainly not for money for I never charged. Most certainly not for reputation because I was established and did not need self-aggrandisement. Could they also speak in a foreign language, unknown to them, not just odd sentences, but information which proved the identity of the communicator and their relationship to the recipient?

At one seance, the husband of Mary Nemtzoglou, an International Spiritualist Federation council member visiting Stansted, spoke to his wife in their native tongue. They were Greek. Mr Nemtzoglou was not quite fully materialised, but Mary recognised both his build and voice. He told her he would remove threads from her clothing as a reminder that he had been there with her and also spoke about his son in Athens.

Mary's husband stood about nine feet from the cabinet and was seen standing besides me. Medium Margaret Pearson sat to one side of the cabinet. She is just about the most practical and honest person I know. Margaret would not say that a thing happened if there was any possibility of it being wrong. Mary checked afterwards...and she did find threads missing from her skirt in a place that one could not see.

Not all our seances were successful. I remember one in the early part of 1981, again at Barbie's flat. We were due to meet some months previously, but I was involved in a car accident and so didn't get there. We had arranged for infra-red camera equipment as we hoped for materialisation, but it was not to be. The ectoplasm flowed, but the conditions were hot and sticky and things didn't work out as we had hoped. It was to be the last chance of this kind because Barbie, my good friend of so many years, passed in the summer of 1981.

Another seance which went wrong was in the summer of 1976. It was most peculiar; the seance was quite normal in the library at Stansted Hall. There were about 80 people. I had entranced, and the ectoplasm was emerging.

Cuckoo had started to speak when apparently there was a loud click. The ectoplasm immediately withdrew and I was burned, not seriously thank goodness, but with quite a nasty burn around my solar plexus. I left and went to my room. Clairaudient Doris Stokes was present. As she had been a nurse, Doris followed me and was able to check that it didn't need treatment, but she said she thought I had high blood pressure as well.

Tape-recorders had been used at previous seances, but always with the permission and knowledge of the guides. Of course, we never found out just what happened and can only assume that this was the cause, but it illustrates the danger present at every demonstration of physical mediumship where you allow people in on trust. It may be that static electricity had built up in the room. The guides said it was some form of radiation, but you can only take so many precautions when you demonstrate to a crowd.

I, along with other mediums, have often been accused by sceptics of secreting muslin or such about our persons or even swallowing the stuff only to regurgitate or produce it during the seance. If so, how then is it dry to the touch? How then can the material be soft at one moment and hard the next? These sceptics ignore the variety of textures, the density and the speed with which it moves from one location to the next.

What vast quantities of material would have to be used and manipulated in the dark to produce the results of just one successful sitting, one where normally people are sitting so close that they could, with little difficulty, reach out and touch me as at Barbie's flat. There, two sitters were one on either side of me, holding my hands.

One person, a scientist called Dr Colvin, instigated a most dreadful story in the national papers. He and a brigadier, who also belonged to the Society for Psychical Research, said one of my seances was a cheat. Dr Colvin stated that he searched the library at Stansted Hall before a seance and found yards of material hidden in my chair.

Neither he nor the paper in question offered any explanation of why he had not complained at the time and waited four years before releasing this accusation. If he had discovered material secreted in my chair, why did he not draw the attention of the people present to this fact at the time?

Dr Colvin did not offer an explanation of how the material was manipulated. The materialised forms often move yards away from where I am seated; they float above the head and sometimes seem to just disappear, as if into a hole in the floor. He did not mention any equipment which would, presumably, have to be used in order to produce shapes and movement.

Anyone who knows Stansted Hall also knows that the floors are solid and that any such hole for ectoplasm to disappear into would be immediately obvious. It is not only my integrity in question when these accusations are made, but also the integrity of the people who organise and those who witness the event.

During the seance, Dr Colvin was invited to feel the ectoplasm and had declared to all present that it had a gauze-like texture. If he was going to make a statement four years later to national papers, then it would have been better had he said so at the time.

Well-known Spiritualist Peter Parnham was present at this session and made a statement in my defence. It was his mother's materialised form that was one of those "bits of cloth." Peter resented the implications that first I was a cheat, and then that he and all those present were so gullible as to be fooled by such methods.

He pointed out that his mother had given intimate personal evidence of her identity, and that as she came away from the cabinet he and his sister remarked how tall she was. The control said that was because they had not materialised her legs. Once this was done, she assumed her normal proportions of some four feet ten inches. The form did not come back into the cabinet for this adjustment, but it was made there and then.

Incidentally, the seance was taped. Peter ordered a copy after the seance as Dr Colvin was offering them for sale. When he received it some time afterwards his mother's speech was not on the tape. You can imagine that when all this came out I felt quite sick. Spirit have been so good to me over the years, but they are powerless to protect me from the venom in this sort of affair. Incidentally, after a lengthy investigation, the verdict of a tribunal to investigate allegations after I demonstrated in Bristol was "Not proven."

I was so very upset at Dr Colvin's claims. They came when the union was holding its annual general meeting. Distraught, I just could not attend the Sunday of conference after reading of the accusations in a Sunday paper. It had surely been timed just for this! I was ashamed that my name should be so used; I was ashamed that Spiritualism should be so smeared. I was actually frightened of the support that I knew I should get from our members. I didn't want to risk breaking down. And I truly felt that I might.

I cannot say how it hurts me when I read of such things. I do not gain materially. Such events as materialisation seances do not even enhance my ego for I know nothing of them other than that which is relayed to me afterwards. Even photographs are not proof for the sceptic.

The Spiritualist papers picked up the story and printed it. I was cross at the time, but then I was going through a very bad patch. I had been threatened physically. Bomb threats were sent to my church and my home. I was ready to give up altogether. Good friends defended me, Spirit stayed close, but it was a difficult time and I cannot forget these sort of things.

Spirit forms who are both larger and smaller than me have materialised over the years, sometimes more than one at the same time! I am trying to be honest here. Not all have been recognised by their features, but many have. This is something that cannot be done by trickery. Above all is the evidence that they present, the personal information, the little matters like a father's braces which were always falling down help in their recognition.

All these are part of the signs and wonders permitted to us from the spirit world not just to show us that we go on, but that our love links do not die: they are always there for us. It is some time now since I have sat just for materialisation. My health does not permit this these days.

I don't believe anything is right for those who are determined not to believe; they will believe what they want to believe. I have risked my health and strength over the years. Materialisation mediumship does produce changes in the body during the production of ectoplasm. This can — and often does — have an effect on the biological balance of the body and can be detrimental to the medium.

The sceptic cries "Fraud!" They produce magicians who by trickery can produce "phenomena." They risk nothing for if they do not prove fraud they merely state that the medium is "too clever." Their world is flat: they do not see the wonder of the Master. Their minds are closed: they do not accept the glorious diversity and splendour of the works of God.

I would not change the work I have done except perhaps to make it better. I have been very privileged to be the instrument through which many have found comfort, hope and strength.

Chapter 11

TV OR NOT TV?

OVER the years I have had many invitations to appear on television, but I do not like the way that they consider mediums.

It is almost as if we are a peep show. Frankly, I do not think that our work is taken seriously in the media.

The problem is, of course, that the people filming the programme may well be very sincere, but the finished result does not always reflect well upon us as a movement. What I have done is given permission for filming to take place in the location of a church or a centre, sometimes in our college at Stansted.

In 1969 I appeared on a "Women Today" programme. I can't think why they didn't choose a lady medium, but they said they wanted me. Perhaps they felt that women like to see gentlemen! It was filmed at my church at Longton and was quite good, except that they introduced me as a "High Priest"! I had over one thousand letters after that programme.

It did also highlight a common phenomenon. One Birmingham reporter stated that he refused to accept a mind without a body and condemned the programme whilst refusing to even watch it!

When Granada TV featured Doris Stokes giving clairvoyance at Lancaster and Morecombe I allowed them to film a naming service conducted by me afterwards. It was that of George and Madge Dobson and Mr Stokes in 1970. This excited tremendous interest because few people outside our movement realise we have a ceremony like this.

There are so many difficulties involved in these type of productions. I agreed to work for the BBC again in 1972. After an hour's demonstration — during which I gave nine messages — the producers came up to me, saying: "We have a problem. All the messages were given to people who were out of range of the cameras and microphones. Could you give just one more message to someone in the front seats where they can be filmed?"

Well, I wanted to help, but the energy levels were now rather low. Jim Duffield, who was chairing, said it would not be possible, but I thought it might be. I sat quietly and we all concentrated. Then Spirit came again to my side and I knew that it was right. I was able to give a lady several names and an address which she accepted as correct. After that there was no stopping the communicators; they spoke of many friends who were also in Spirit and then a Bet who had just passed in a mining accident. She was so pleased and, of course, so were the TV people.

This was the first time they had filmed a two-hour meeting, and it was very good. It was a programme called "Look East," shown on Anglian TV. The meeting was part of a campaign which we arranged throughout the country in conjunction with "Psychic News." Editor Maurice Barbanell gave the address.

He and I were interviewed afterwards along with four of the recipients who testified to their messages' correctness. There was a funny sequel to this. Free copies of "Psychic News" had been delivered to local homes together with the leaflet, "The Implications of Spiritualism," to publicise the meetings. This led to the Dean of Norwich being asked on the radio's "Epilogue" what he knew about Spiritualism. He replied he knew nothing, but that it was dangerous!

Barbie gave me the same message, well similar, before I left Norwich to travel back to Stansted on the Sunday evening. Well, it was not exactly that Spiritualism was dangerous, but that I was running into danger from Spiritualism.

"You are doing too much," he cautioned, "and tiring yourself out. You will become a spirit description if you don't take more care of your body." Spiritualism can be dangerous if you work so hard that you run yourself into the grave! Of course, he was wrong. And I expect him to admit this when we meet up again on the Other Side as he passed first.

I have to admit there have been some disastrous appearances of people on television. Workers accept the challenge to work in front of magicians or before studio audiences who are just out for a good laugh. The conditions are not right. Spirit do not have a chance to show their true power.

At the time of writing, we have just had a programme made just for us. It was on national TV on BBC 2's "Open Space." The difference is that we specified the conditions of work and the content of the programme. That is very different. Again, the union's Publicity Committee is being asked to make serious comment on psychic and spiritual matters. It is the time for us to move more into the open, just as our workers did in the larger halls so many years ago. But it must be on our terms.

Chapter 12

ANIMALS AND THE AFTERLIFE

THERE are some people who doubt that animals go on to survive death. But we Spiritualists know different. There was a competition in "Psychic News" some years ago. They wanted to know which readers had the best irrefutable evidence that animals do survive death.

The contest was won by S. Brough, of Allen Street, Cheadle who gave his witness after attending one of my seances in 1972 at Stansted Hall when a materialised dog was recognised. The pet was asked to perform a favourite trick by its owner...and immediately jumped from the medium's knee into the air, turning a somersault before landing on the ground in front of the cabinet. The owner later explained that she would throw a piece of sugar in the air; the dog would catch this and then turn a somersault, just as the materialised animal did.

I have very often described and even named animals in demonstrations. Often they come back and show themselves to just add that extra evidence of identity and the communicator names them for me. I have known people cry on realising that a beloved pet is not lost forever, but will be there to love in the spirit world as they were in life.

Once when I was working with psychic artist Coral Polge, I was able to bring a boy to speak with his mother, a Mrs Lilian Dack. The lad was able to give her name, which made identification so much easier. He went on to supply his father's and his grandfather's names. All this proved his memory of earth. Next he described a Highland Terrier which his grandmother had brought to the house just that week. His mother knew by this small fact that her son was truly still around, that he was near her still and able to share in her life. It was such a joy to her to know this.

Sometimes animals are used almost as symbols to give a name without sound. I remember once I was quite bemused to see a birdcage, but no birds in it. I was quite puzzled, but decided to give just what I was getting. The recipient's name was Bird. Another time I saw pigeons. Again, this was not a vision of the creature but a clue. The recipient lived in Pigeon Walk!

I am not very often asked to do healing because, of course, I am not known particularly for this. Sometimes I have been asked to give healing to animals and been pleased on being able to help. I remember one time when a lady approached me about her elderly poodle. This animal was much-loved, but had a heart condition. Then it dislocated a knee joint and was in agony. Of course, the vet could not help because of the heart and advised "putting her down." I was able to help — and the poodle recovered to spend more earth time with her owner.

It is not always necessary to be there in person to help. There was an excellent animal sanctuary at Halesowen in the Midlands. A very loving lady called Mrs Hussen from there contacted me one day about a little Collie called Patch. He had kidney failure. Again, the vet wanted to put him down.

Mrs Hussen called me, but I could not go so promised to send out absent healing. Within two days that little dog was able to eat and drink normally. Further tests showed that his kidneys were functioning normally. The vet thought it was a miracle. But miracles are a one off experience...and healing works all the time!

Chapter 13

TRAINING MEDIUMS

AS I see it, the spirit has gone out of Spiritualism; it is all too often just not there. Once inspiration goes out, then the Spirit cannot stay. With trance mediumship we get such a close contact with the Spirit and are moved by their power. Not all mediums will be deep trance, but a true medium can develop some level of this type of work. We need to get our mediums more in contact with the spirit and our congregations to be spiritualised.

If we can get the movement more aware of the presence of Spirit, then I think we will be able to get in contact with higher powers. Until we do that, we are just people who have found something wonderful, but not using it intelligently.

I am sure that Spirit are guiding us gently back to this realisation. In the past we had wonderful guides like Red Cloud, Silver Birch and White Eagle who were able to share their wisdom with us. We need to be looking to developing mediums once again who can act as channels for these sort of guides. We need to bring that back; there has never been anything written like the teachings of Silver Birch. He was a personality so very different from his medium, Maurice Barbanell.

Mediumship is not of the same standard as fifty years ago, but I do not believe it is because we do not have the mediums. I think that it is in the training that the problem arises. It is in the churches where people go for training that there is a lack of teachers; people with ability, who know the subject and know exactly what to do. We have to realise that in days gone by there were lots more mediums, people who seemed to be born with the gift. Today we do not seem to have these people available.

I think that before people go into training classes they should have a study course where they can be taught the mechanics of mediumship and certainly what they themselves are. We need to know what we ourselves comprise of, the various vehicles of expression within ourselves; the difference between our physical body, the etheric body and the many other bodies which are all together and bound by the powers of Spirit.

We need to take people aside, begin to teach them and give them instruction on how we are made up, what our make up is. That the spirit world is around us, that we are living in worlds within worlds.

When they have completed their study, then their teacher should be capable of taking them into the next step, which I believe to be a spiritual one, of learning how to blend with God. A link with God and Spirit can be achieved through periods of meditation. Potential mediums need a teacher who has learned about meditation, who can take them through that next stage.

Of course, it may be that there is no person close to them who will be able to do this. This makes development very difficult. There are very few books which are useful for training in this way. These must be brought up to date. We, the Spiritualists' National Union, hope to provide pamphlets to help.

The union does provide study courses through correspondence. We are now providing very good practical courses at our college which are designed for the serious student.

First they become aware, making effort to acquire knowledge. This is a vital basis for expansion of the self. Then they move on to the initial practical stages before enrolling in the more intense development and the advanced courses that are now being offered.

Eventually we hope to have centres all over the country, but we must have people who are capable of training others in this way. They must understand what is needed by the developing medium.

Once people are aware of their real self, they talk about God and Spirit and love, but few really know the true meaning of what they are saying. They can learn about mediumship when they have this understanding. If we could only teach people that God is Spirit and power, and that we must blend with God because mediumship is, in my opinion, a calling. We cannot develop it properly unless we feel this urge within ourself, something that makes it vital that we go forward. That calling must be from God and Spirit.

Before we begin our development, we should look at our spiritual self first. We move away from the intellectual to knowledge and wisdom. We need to have the psychic ability, but the Spirit must be paramount, the realisation that we are of God. Mediums must be prepared for development so that they can move away from this material world and onto a higher level to be able to understand the spiritual as separate from the material. This is why it is so important that they first feel the call within themselves. How else will they find the strength and determination needed for development?

I believe that in the early stages of development there must be a medium available who has vision. When we have good people who are to be trained they must first have set out on a journey, to have learned about the spiritual. It is only then that a good medium will be able to see where they should be encouraged to engage their attentions. It is at this stage there must be a sorting out.

There are some who will not be able to get far — and the teacher should be honest. They must discern the purpose of why people want to develop. I was very lucky, you see. When I was a child, I saw Spirit quite clearly and listened to their voices. I was already a medium. I communicated. I listened to people who I didn't believe had passed over. I believed they were very real people. I had a very wonderful mother who knew I would play my part. She taught me from a very early age that I must be willing to give and not to take. She made me aware that it was a question of developing my work to serve mankind, not putting the material side first but the spiritual.

When I see a potential medium, I look to see whether they are willing to put serving of mankind first. Once I know they have this in their hearts, I also know that God can call them to any level, to any standard.

Many people complain that Spiritualism and mediumship are not as good as they once were. They do not see that we have learned from and expanded upon the past, that life is different now. Families were more closely linked. There was not the noise, bustle and speed there is now. I also believe that Spirit were breaking through then: they knew the need for Spirit to be "felt" and so mediums were born to play their part when the conditions were right for their development as Spirit wanted it.

People were together more then. There seemed to be a greater comradeship, and a stronger friendship. Spiritualism and mediumship are different now, but that is right as we are living in a different age. We have lost some things, but gained others.

I don't believe the circles they held 50 or 60 years ago were as advanced as they are today; I don't think we should be teaching people to pray and link in advanced classes. I believe this must be done in the early stages. If we want to talk to God, then this is something very private, and should be practised daily. A good medium is perceptive and will learn by observation and experience how to pray in public. When you go to development class, all the time that is available should be devoted to the training of your mediumship and the ability to use the right vehicle for your mediumship. A medium's life is prayer. No medium can be a first class medium until they have experienced the deep silence and felt the presence of God through prayer.

I think that materialism is very strong because of the way the whole world has become imprisoned by it over the years. It has become a way of life. Spiritualism is really the balancing of that; it is dealing with the spiritual side of man's nature, encouraging people to understand that there are worlds within worlds. That this material world will vanish away; that the body, too, will vanish.

The things that are visible are illusion: the real things are the invisible. Spiritualism must teach that above all things. We seem to have lost this. We are more involved in the materialism. I think that this is a pity. We must teach people to develop not for gain but for the spiritual. I think that is where the whole idea of development lies.

Clairaudience can only be developed by people who are mediums because it involves sounds and vibrations which are coming from higher levels which are divorced from the world as we know it. The fallacy has come from the past where people believed that clairaudience is heard by the physical ears, but, of course, it is not. We have learnt more since then as we have studied our mediumship. Clairaudience is part of the sixth sense.

I am clairaudient. When my mother realised I had this gift, she decided to make me very aware of it. She used to put cotton wool in my ears and bind them so I couldn't hear physical sounds at all. She made me sit for spiritual development like that and listen to spirit voices which did not come from this world at all. I used to have a throat problem which became very dry so I drank a lot of water. I began to realise that the sounds were not coming to my ears, but to my throat. I also realised it was my voice box that was being used when I was clairaudient. I learnt a great deal from that experience.

When we are watching a medium who is developing, we have to be aware of where the power is building and where the light is. If it is round the throat, then we know we have someone who will develop clairaudience and that they must be developed in a way to ensure that they will learn to use the gift correctly. I have learned from the past by studying my own mediumship and how my gifts work in relation to the way that it was taught to me.

Many mediums fail to develop their gifts fully because they are not aware of the possibilities. All mediums are born with an awakened sixth sense, which is a spiritual one. There is tremendous difference between clairvoyance which is psychic to clairvoyance which is pure mediumship. To be clairvoyant, you must develop soul power for the manifestation of Spirit to take place and the vision to come to you. You have to learn that we are receivers. You have to learn the difference between the psychic, that deals mostly with mind and sensitivity, and communication where we are dealing with separate minds of Spirit which have to blend on other levels of awareness and consciousness. Now we are setting about trying to guide people for today's conditions.

Clairvoyance can be used on two levels. You can be a clairvoyant without being a medium. The psychic can be a clairvoyant, but is not necessarily a medium. By mediumship we are talking about people who are in communication with the minds of people who have passed from this earth life.

The psychic is one who has become sensitive to environment, sensitive to situations that people are involved with and can occasionally find some answers to the problems with which people are faced. When considering mediumship, we are dealing with

Spirit, which must first prove that man is a spiritual being, that when the physical body dies, our other body lives on and takes its place in this other world, which is a world within this one.

I have thought a great deal about this and this is the way that I see clairvoyance. There is the clairvoyance where we can tell people what we see about the situation around them, but this is limited. If we make contact with the spirit world and use our mediumship onto the level of clairvoyance, we have vision, very clear vision, which is able to show us the situation with the person as they are, but also the situation of the person as they will be. This is not limited in the same way.

We are able to look ahead to see clearly the way in which the life of the person will go. We are filled with thoughts that come to us from a much higher level than the physical or psychic level, a level from a much higher dimension of life. That is a wonderful experience. The medium must then be trained to interpret what they see. That *is* clairvoyance.

I believe prediction is possible, but by a medium. I have my doubts whether this is possible by a psychic, at least on a regular basis; sometimes they can be a hundred per cent accurate, but on the next visit they are not. When you go to a medium who is able to move onto this higher level, they should be able to know what is written. Not because of destiny, but because it is known.

When we receive communication from the spirit world, they fill us with knowledge, ideas and thought; this comes to us as a picture. Through experience we learn how to interpret it. The reliability depends very much on the level from which the communication is given. No medium should give information until they are sure Spirit are there and that they are working on this higher level.

We must be in communication with other worlds, with dimensions where there is truth. This is why I emphasise the importance of development. We must focus on our experience. I have learned a great deal by looking at my own mediumship. I have been working for over sixty years now and learned a lot in that time.

It is always better to have an individual sitting rather than a message in a public demonstration. Some mediums will work better in one sphere, some in the other, although I like both. But I don't like to be rushed into a sitting or a public performance. I like to be prepared for either.

My work has been primarily for publicity in larger halls. I can get across to the public because I have developed my powers for this purpose. I am able, within a very short time, to be aware of the spirit world because I provide the means by which they can appear to me. That means I have learned how to get over the barrier of what I call the psychic to communicate clearly with the spirit world.

Then, all at once, the whole building is alive, alive with the spirit world. I make the bridge whereby we can move from one level of consciousness to the other. When you have to take a private sitting, you have first of all to become sensitive to the sitter, but at the same time need to have an enormous amount of love and soul power.

You must never try to confuse a sitting which is a purely psychic one to that which is a spiritual one. I am more involved with the spiritual sittings. I like to create powerful conditions where those from the Higher Realm can manifest to my spiritual vision.

I like to feel the presence of those who have worked with me over many years from the spirit world, and I know then that my sitting is going to be a success. I know that if I get caught up in things that don't seem to be correct that I can blend for a moment with those spirit helpers who have more knowledge than me and get some of the answers.

A good medium should be able to work with both private sitters and public demonstrations. All the people I have trained in my church have been instructed into how to give private sittings because I believe this is excellent training for public work.

Then there are other forms of sensitivity, like automatic writing.

This is a rare gift. A person who has this talent must be specially trained. Some years ago we had quite a few people who had this faculty and were trained, but there do not seem to be so many now.

There is a difference between a person who is inspired and wants to write things down, but this is not automatic writing. With automatic writing, you are used only as a vessel, as a medium. Your hand is used by Spirit. It by-passes you. Spirit use your hand to write out their message. The medium who has this gift should be trained away from the developing circle with one or two people at the most to bring the gift forward and to find out who is using the medium for that purpose. They must carry out any instructions given from the spirit world.

Psychometry has always interested me because my mother trained me as a psychometrist. I have found it of tremendous help in developing as a sensitive. In the early stages of mediumship, that sensitivity has to be developed. Then we can become sensitive to vibrations beyond psychometry, onto higher levels. Even mediums like myself who are born mediums have to go through various levels so we can come to an understanding and learn to use our powers accordingly.

It is a gift; to become a good psychometrist needs a lot of development. Psychometry is the history, the thoughts, feelings and ambitions of the person who has handled the article. It is more or less the character of the person. When you take an article and psychometrise it, you must begin with the present and then build the character of the owner of the object. Then you gradually move into the past.

I remember my mother providing me with an article which had been brought from Egypt. It was a piece of stone. She asked me first who had brought it, not what it was, but who had handled it last. I was able to build the image of the man and his character. I was not able to get his name, but did get a very good description of him. Next Mother wanted me to find out where he was when he had handled the stone, and I was able to see him in Egypt. The process was gradual, over several weeks. Each time I started at the beginning. Eventually I could by-pass that and deal with other things that I did not know about with this man.

The person who is going to be a psychometrist should be trained individually. It takes time and patience. When you are trained in this way, you don't have to rely on the spirit world for everything. When a sitter comes into the room, you automatically know what they have come for. You don't have to use energies in that direction, but can concentrate on your work as a medium, on communication with the spirit world. Psychometry should only be used correctly. It has nothing to do with the future, only to do with the present and past.

I remember a gentleman some years ago who asked me to come and look at some land. He was a friend of our family, and wanted to know what to do with the land. Well, I "saw" houses and roads and told him so. He was disappointed because he wanted to use it for a different purpose, but, you see, I psychometrised the land, then I used my mediumship to move beyond the present into that timeless world beyond the now! Only an experienced medium is capable of such detail. It was not to be for some ten years, but I was right. I knew what he wanted, that he needed to know what would happen to the land and didn't fiddle about with the present.

Though sometimes asked about pendulums, I am not well acquainted with them. I believe they can be influenced through the mind, and am always worried about those things that can be so influenced by the mind, like the table. My mother used the pendulum and had some very good results, but I have never been very interested in this.

Turning to the ouija board, I have known some who achieved very good results in the past. It is not something that should be encouraged, unless perhaps by those who have a gift for automatic writing or can be taken over by the Spirit in a form of trance where the hand can be used.

As with all things, it depends upon why we use it and how. In the wrong hands I believe it should not be used because it can be influenced by the mind. The person may be very sincere, but I think the mind benders who do all sorts of things with metal objects have proved to us that the mind can have a very powerful influence. This is not always realised.

I am quite convinced about astrology. Again, it depends on the way that we use it. If we use it just for fortune-telling or as a joke then that is not correct. But if we use it for its mystic influence and for its real purpose in life then I can assure you that it plays its part extremely well. I have done many courses of astrology. By using aura reading and psychometry, with the knowledge of astrology I have found a strong relationship between them. I have been able to look at a person and just by what I have "seen" even find the date, month and sign of which they have been born. I have asked an astrologer and they've been able to interpret the same things as I have to a person.

Many Spiritualists will not look at other forms of sensitivity, but I have always had an intense curiosity about life and the abilities which are there but not always used. I do not necessarily use these myself. Indeed, I very seldom have time now to even explore other energies, but they are part of life; they have a part to play in the great pattern.

There are a number of people who use different ways of focusing their attention and thus gain access to their sensitivity. My mother was a very good palmist, but I do not know that she knew the lines or anything. She used the hand as a focus for concentration and in that she had vision.

When you use these sort of gifts but cannot communicate with the spirit world, it is merely a question of trying to find what lies in the future. In fact, it is really fortune-telling because you are looking to the future and to advise people of the good and the bad that might be there. I think that these things — palms, tea leaves, cards — are used as a means of concentration. They are psychic gifts, not spiritual gifts. The difference is that the spiritual gift is vision, where we are in contact with people of higher spiritual levels.

I am not opposed to psychism, but it does not prove Spiritualism; it does not prove that there are worlds within worlds. I am more interested in teaching people about a way of life — that this world is a wonderful place, but is only a starting off place to the future where life continues. I think that only Spiritualism can give this to us. It takes us to the very centre of all life, which is God. Without the knowledge and proof of Spiritualism, there is no meaning to life.

What, then, is a medium? I like the word vessel as it seems to sum up what a medium is. We have to be very careful that the medium does not try to manufacture the spirit world, in other words to force it through. Many people said in the past that we "call up the dead." We have to be very careful we don't do that.

I think many circles in the past sat for the purpose of calling the spirit world to them. This is the wrong approach. The idea of a medium is first of all to realise that we have to tune in to what is known as the etheric world. Many people who investigate Spiritualism do so with the express purpose of finding out, how to make contact with someone who has passed over, to find out if there is life after death; if there is a purpose to life.

Before this can happen we have to develop the means, the senses, to communicate with those who have passed on. Therefore, the medium must be trained to be able to get away from this dimension of life, which is the material world, and raise their consciousness onto another level where their senses are on a much quicker frequency and where this other world is. This is essential, to allow the other world to come to us in vision form.

The student must learn how to ascend away from the physical onto this other dimension, the etheric world. Although they are still here, they are able to use their senses in that dimension. As a vessel, they can become filled with the information that Spirit are pouring out to them. They become receivers and are filled, not with preconceived ideas or by telling Spirit what to do or say. They then have to learn how to interpret signs and wonders. They are voicing the feelings and thoughts of those who have come to them, as they have become a channel for this information from the higher level.

The ability to interpret is vital. We must — and do — develop the spiritual aspect all the time. How can anyone pour out the love of a child if you are not a lover of children? How can you convey the love of an animal if you detest animals? You can only receive what you are capable of understanding.

You see how important it is that you develop with the right material when you become this vessel and become aware of this other world and its people. They are living, vibrant people who are trying to tell you how lovely it is that someone at last knows they are alive. You are waiting there, ready and free to capture every living vibrant moment.

When you have it, you must give it as you feel it. So you must be prepared to live the feeling, to live in all kinds of conditions and be able to understand all levels of consciousness or levels of mind so you are passing on what you have received without anything coming from yourself, without allowing your own subconscious mind to colour what you have been given. You must not jump to conclusions, but try and give it just as you have received it...with love.

The whole idea of trance is that the message is not given through a second person, the medium being the second person. It is the projection of the spirit person through the medium — and they don't want the medium to interfere. This is why the unconscious state is vital. This is, of course, very difficult, but nevertheless there have been wonderful mediums in the past, and today a few, who can go into this unconscious state so that the personality of Spirit can come through. Here the medium is indeed a pure vessel whereby only the word of spirit comes through.

Those who have this gift must be trained so they go deeper into the unconscious state so they can be taken over and the projection of spirit come through. Their world, their ideas, their feelings and words can come through direct. It is a wonderful form of mediumship. I only wish we had more people with the gift of full or deep trance. Clairaudience, even clairvoyance, is wonderful for us, but you can well see that the message is always through another person. The medium is the bridge. But with trance it is direct from Spirit.

There are mediums that have provided the direct voice and can be in the normal state of consciousness while working. But if you follow them, as I have done, you find that in the early stages of development they were a deep trance medium. They have to be to allow these powers and this particular form of mediumship to function.

The etheric voice box of the medium is used together with ectoplasm. These two are brought together by the power of spirit. The trumpet is often used to enhance and increase the volume of the sound. Physical mediumship is such a long and intricate subject that a whole book would be needed really to cover the subject in depth.

Trance mediumship is the basis of all forms of physical mediumship. Direct voice is a magnificent example. Those who possess it have to be developed by the link from the Spirit. They really do the work. We really do very little; we provide the conditions. It is work that is direct from the spirit world. Today we should be concentrating on this kind of mediumship. I think it is a great pity we don't.

It is only because there is a lack of knowledge, a lack of teaching. It is a gift that is very essential, a magnificent gift. How on earth are we going to have the advice from those greater minds in the spirit world unless we have available people here who will allow these minds to come through and communicate their knowledge to us? The world needs it now more than ever before. That is why it is important that mediumship as such and the key to mediumship is found.

We must encourage people but so do properly. Don't throw them in without knowledge; don't let them tackle something without knowing with what they are dealing. Don't let them come in unless they have first found God. They must know that all coming through is on a spiritual level, not on a purely psychic level.

All these things are necessary. I believe that if we can do this, put our house in order and make Spiritualism really live then the world will live. We will find that a light will come upon our earth. We will fear no future as we fear it today because we are in safe hands if we are in the real hands of the spirit world.

There is a very definite relationship between Spiritualism and spirituality. I have been very concerned about spirituality, especially when people become mediums. I believe that before mediums develop their gifts they should be trained through meditation and spiritual awareness. I cannot emphasise this enough! I believe that development comes last. I think preparation is the important key because unless we maintain the spiritual standard I have spoken of, the work deteriorates as time goes on.

This has been one of the problems of many of our mediums, unfortunately. They have reached a level and never tried to get higher. They have kept to that one level and merely looked at it from a material point of view rather than a spiritual one. Egotism is a problem, but if we deal with spiritual growth first, we can perhaps eradicate this problem. Fame and fortune have always been hazards in Spiritualism. The answer is that we must never lose sight of the virtue of humility.

Chapter 14

MY GREATEST LOVE

LOOKING back, as I see things, my life's work has been about three things. The first was ordained clearly: I would be a medium. The second and third were less clearly defined by Spirit and yet events have been so obviously manipulated from the other world that I cannot doubt they are involved, and that my life has been as it was intended.

It may be I have not always done things as I should have. There are some things I might well alter if I were given the chance, but I believe I have done my best and have followed my inner spiritual direction.

Stansted Hall has been my greatest love, I think even beyond the union. I see in the SNU an instrument which, if properly developed, will take Spiritualism throughout the world. I see in the hall the dreams of our pioneers. I have worked over these years to make these dreams a reality.

Perhaps, yes, of course, I am right in saying, that the one must compliment the other. The fact that in one I find duty and in the other a dream does not denigrate either; I have worked, given my life for both. Man is the stuff of which his dreams are made.

My involvement with Stansted began before the hall belonged to the union. It started with its then owner, Arthur Findlay.

This was a very great man to whom the Spiritualist movement owes a debt of gratitude not only for the classic books written about Spiritualism, but also for his last gift to us — Stansted Hall, which houses the Arthur Findlay College.

He believed it was very necessary to take across the world the message of Spiritualism; that there is a continuation of life after death; that there is no cessation of life at all, but a continuation.

I am sure he had no idea when he bought Stansted Hall to house his family that one day he would hand it over to the Spiritualist movement. I think that even then Spirit were bringing a future reality into the realms of possibility.

It may seem to us, who have visited this magnificent old mansion, that it was rather large for just three people, but in those days people like Arthur lived in such style.

I remember the first time I heard Arthur Findlay. This was in Brighton many years ago following the union's conference. He gave a fine address. I was very impressed with what he had to say upon the subject of Spiritualism. He was a marvellous character, giving his words a life of their own.

I did not know — or even dream — at that time that one day I would be invited to his home. It was about two years before his passing. I received a message that he wished to see me. I do not pretend for one moment that I did not guess why as I was becoming very well known as a medium.

I think now that I did not realise the whole of his purpose. I think he "knew" I would be important to his ideal for even then he had dreams of the future. Perhaps he recognised that without my intervention, the conservative element within the union would have their way and the Arthur Findlay College would not have a chance for a successful future.

Obviously I was a little nervous for Arthur was a very strong character. He was not a man who played around. Mr Findlay knew just what he wanted — and either liked or really disliked you. There was no in between. And he was not frightened to express his opinions!

He was, after all, a very successful business man who had, through his own efforts, made his mark in the world. Arthur had written many books about Spiritualism and was very respected. Mr Findlay was a founder of the International Institute for Psychical Research and, among many other positions, was invited to become an Honorary Vice-President of the SNU.

By then, I had a car and drove down in it. I still remember my first car with affection. I called her "Lydia," and only parted reluctantly with her when my firm insisted on my having a replacement.

I drove into Stansted village and asked how to get to the hall. I had to go to where there were two gates and then up the drive. It seemed a very long way up the drive to the hall. I was very impressed, especially when I came to the courtyard where I had to park my car.

I came from a good, but quite humble background, so it seemed marvellous to me that someone, a family, actually lived in such a magnificent place. Even from the outside there was this air of splendour, a remoteness which seemed to be separate from and yet curiously a part of the surrounding countryside. Perhaps it was a sense of timelessness.

I was a little early and so decided to wait there as I was sure Mr Findlay was a man who would not want you there before the appointed time. It was a beautiful day so a pleasure to sit there, although I kept a check upon the time as I was also sure he wouldn't appreciate lateness.

I rang the bell right on 2 o'clock and was taken in. I passed through this wonderful gallery with the impressive staircase to my left and great pictures hanging upon the walls. For me it was quite awe-inspiring. I have always enjoyed beautiful things...and there was beauty all around me.

The atmosphere seemed to me to be highly charged. I could feel the spirituality, the peace. There were flowers everywhere. The furniture gleamed. As I looked through the enormous windows I could see how well the grounds were kept.

It was quite an experience for me. I have never forgotten that first impression of quiet, elegant spirituality which seemed to me to pervade the whole atmosphere. In spite of my being slightly over-awed, I could not help but be impressed and quietened.

The man who let me in took me through to the study. I did wonder whether this was a butler, the kind I had seen on films where they open the front door and attend "below." I found out later that he was not, but it did create this impression upon me.

Arthur was waiting for me. We exchanged greetings. After we had spoken together for some time, he asked me if I would give him a sitting. I did.

I was able to bring forward many people who had long passed

into the world of spirit. Mr Findlay was able to share their tremendous love for him, their memories of times together and other evidence.

He was very pleased with what I was able to give him. We then had tea together during which he spoke to me about his plans and dreams for the hall as a place of teaching and learning. Arthur told me he wanted to give this beautiful house to Spiritualism — and he felt the Spiritualists' National Union would be best able to manifest his vision.

As I drove away, my head was full of all this. I couldn't help wondering if the union would be able to fulfil his dreams that Stansted should become a school for mediums. He wanted a principal with training and teaching staff, and that it should be kept solely for that purpose.

I seriously doubted if this was possible because I had some small idea of the cost of such a venture. Arthur's idea was that it should be maintained on a small level, with no more than twenty or twenty-five students at a time. I often wonder just what he thought as he saw his idea growing and expanding.

Mr Findlay really wanted it used for those who had proved they had mediumistic powers, that they would be there for further training before going out into the country to prove survival.

When the time came and he passed into the world of spirit and the union was to take on this task there were a lot of difficulties which he had not envisaged. Arthur had intended to leave more money to help with the upkeep, but most of this was lost to us one way and another. It was most unfortunate as the lack of money made everything so much more difficult.

I was not really very important in the union at that time. I was not on the council or even involved at local, district level. I had achieved a reputation as a medium because of my close contact with Spirit and my ability to pass on what they were saying clearly. My style had attracted a great deal of attention.

My time was taken up with my church where I was president and where I had a lot to do and, of course, travelling around the country as a medium. In between all this I had to earn a living. So I was kept very busy and had no thoughts of working in the administration.

I was actually quite surprised when invited to become the Class 'B' representative and be on the National Council. As I said, I had never worked at district level, the usual route for such invitations. I often wondered, then, why it had all happened. Of course, I can now look back and see that it was all part of a plan.

Arthur Findlay was a committed Spiritualist, but I am sure he had not thought to give his home to his commitment. I was so impressed with Stansted when I first went there, but even I had little thought when I drove up that drive and walked through those doors how many times I would make the same journey over the years.

Indeed, I did not think then that I would be the instrument which would be used to save Stansted Hall for the work for the movement. Yet this is what happened.

Naturally I realised what wonderful potential it had being in quiet surroundings and yet near to the airport which could bring people from all around the world to our door. I felt that British Spiritualism would be the centre of a great expansion, an explosion of spiritual knowledge, which could change the future. I still believe this is so.

Arthur Findlay could not know to what extent he was being used: to buy the place and then to invite mediums to stay there, which he often did; to sit in that wonderful atmosphere and be inspired in writing his books, which are now classics of spiritual knowledge; and finally to hand it all over to the SNU to continue the work he started. Who will dare to say that Spirit did not have a hand in all this? Not I!

I remember how difficult those years were after the union had taken over the hall. We tried to get plans passed so we could use the building for residential purposes. We desperately needed to modernise some of the rooms.

As they stood, they were not suitable. We needed extensive alterations before we could get people to visit and let us have an income. We had such heavy overheads that even we could not believe it at times — and we had to find the money to pay for them!

The Air Ministry had other ideas and didn't want to agree our plans at first. Even then I think they foresaw the development of the existing airport and wanted to make sure there would be no problems with compulsory purchase. Gradually, they changed their mind and decided they didn't want our land.

Because I had been asked to meet Arthur and he shared his dreams with me which I knew were right, I felt I had a responsibility to stand by his wish, one I must help to bring into being. I was certain Spirit were influencing my feelings in this direction, and that it was important I should take heed.

Of course, we had a battle. Half of our members saw the hall as a white elephant, eating up valuable and scarce funds, preventing other important developments taking place over the country.

Some churches had to postpone building plans for one year when money had been given to the hall — and some were understandably cross. They wanted us to sell the hall because they saw this terrible drain on our resources.

The union was going through a very challenging time just then for this was the mid-1960s. We owed a lot of money to the bank. Indeed, we seemed to owe money to everyone! It was quite frightening, and very difficult for us to see a way out of the mess we were in.

It was then I made my decision I would stand by the union, although I didn't know then that it would be, from that time, my life's work!

I had a very wonderful spiritual experience and realised that this was why I had been ordained; that we must go forward and make our recovery so we could take our place and make a mark in the world. I have been very fortunate in my life as Spirit have directed me in all sorts of ways and always proved to be right.

Through sheer hard work and sacrifice by so many great and generous people we have turned the situation around, making a success out of what could so easily have been failure.

I believe I was there to bring Stansted together and make it what it is — a centre where people come for training from all over the world, a place where there is an atmosphere which is conducive to the development of the Spiritualist medium.

Not everyone would have been able to take on this task. I was chosen, I think, first because of my mediumistic capabilities and so I would be able to be the principal to help in training others, and secondly because I was eventually to be the leader of the union and in a position to influence others.

Spiritualists from all over the world now look to Britain. The standard of mediumship in this country is higher than any other place. It important to remember the tremendous responsibility that rests upon our shoulders.

When Arthur Findlay was inspired to hand over this magnificent building to Spiritualism, it was because he recognised the need that there should be a centre of learning, a college for psychic studies. A place where people from all over the world could meet together, to share their knowledge and to understand the truth of spiritual progress.

I do not know if he realised that England would be a Spiritualist centre for the future of mankind, but he did know that England must have its spiritual centre. This building now stands as a monument to the hundred years and more that we have been a movement. We have something here that no one else has got.

We, the union and its members, have kept the hall open in spite of all the heartaches and pain of the years. It stands a credit to Arthur Findlay, and to all the spirit guides and helpers, the mediums, teachers and students, who have worked within its walls.

Here people can meet and receive the evidence from their loved ones that they have not died. Folk from all over come to hear what we have to offer. They go away with more knowledge and understanding about God and life.

When we took over the hall, it was a family home. The facilities were quite primitive. The drains emptied into a cess pit. This was quite adequate for a small household, but would never do for a residential college.

We had to get permission to install proper drainage. Even putting in extra lavatories was a problem. All the floors were stone and concrete and could not be drilled through, but the levels had to be raised to accommodate the pipes.

Some of the bedrooms were divided. One, Arthur's own, actually made three separate rooms! Baths, showers and electricity had to be installed. Beds, bedding, cutlery and china had to be purchased. It sounds so prosaic now, but it all had to be done. Bit by bit, room by room, it was completed. We had to have fire doors fitted as the public were to be resident.

The times I have heard people grumble about those doors! They shut slowly until the last few inches and then suddenly speed up. The resulting "Bang!" wakes up those who have gone to bed early.

In the early days, people had to go along to a little room near the lift to get a cup of tea. As they went through the very heavy doors they had to be careful or else all the tea spilled. Thanks to the Friends of Stansted, all the rooms have their own kettle now so this does not happen.

No one realised just how near the SNU and the Arthur Findlay College came to liquidation. Only three of us knew the whole truth. But I had taken on Arthur Findlay's vision. It had become my own. And I knew it was also the desire of our spirit friends that the college should become a reality.

Because of this vision, I had become intensely interested in the union and realised that the thread which held me to the spirit world was also entwined with the future of the SNU and the hall.

Somehow, they were all related. My presence here on earth had been ordained. Here I faced my destiny. It can be an awesome moment to realise one's destiny. There were times when I despaired, but I never gave up hope.

Chapter 15

A WHITE ELEPHANT?

I HAVE never enjoyed controversy. I prefer a quiet life, but sometimes we are faced with things and then have to decide what is the right thing to do. I have been so lucky. I had a conviction and help!

The year I became the president of the union, veteran Spiritualist Percy Wilson declared that the SNU had only two years to live. Indeed, it seemed to be so at that time for we faced bankruptcy.

It was an awful feeling to take the position as head of an organisation which was on the verge of collapsing. I cannot say I was not worried. I was

The work we had done at Stansted Hall came in for so much criticism for we owed thousands. We had lost money every year since we had opened. In 1964 our income was only £1,352, but expenses were £2,849. By 1969 our income had risen to £17,511, but our expenses increased in ratio.

There seemed to be no winning! The deficit over six years was enormous, standing at £25,669. We had spent over £100,000 on renovations. People said the hall should be sold to clear the debt. I did understand the fears of our members, but even if I had been persuaded to abandon the dream we could not have cleared all we owed by selling. There had to be another solution.

I shared those fears, but I could not let people know for as the new president had to appear very confident even when I felt worried. I wondered what on earth we could do. We discussed all of this at the National Council. I also, as I have said, discussed it all with my friends from the spirit world.

Percy Wilson pointed out that Britten Memorial Trust and the

Arthur Findlay College had the same aims. Emma Hardinge Britten, that great Victorian Spiritualist, had envisaged a School of Prophets. At that time, the union's head office and the British Lyceum Union were both housed in the Britten Trust, which was in Tibbs Lane, Manchester.

The building was wanted by the corporation for redevelopment so we thought, "Why not make Stansted a trust, move the offices there and combine the two?" The Charity Commissioners agreed — and we made the move. We were able to reduce the money owed to the union's Building Fund Pool by a considerable amount.

This was still not enough, although it was a heavy weight off my mind. I started "The Friends of Stansted." We held meetings to raise money. So many people were generous, not just with money, although of that was our immediate priority.

Over the years, the Friends have given so much to the hall. They have renovated furniture, made new curtains, painted, decorated and helped in the gardens. I sometimes wonder just what we could have done without them. I am still on their small committee and I would not want to give up that responsibility.

We had a Garden Party — and raised £560 in one day. That doesn't seem so much today because prices have risen so much over the years, but at that time it was a wonderful amount...and we were able to work wonders with even small donations.

The day was opened by Clark Findlay from Aberdeen. He was Arthur Findlay's nephew. Healer Nan Mackenzie and her husband John donated a Grand Piano, which I played while Frank Tams sang. We did a rendition of "Bless This House," which was very much appreciated. Frank had a splendid voice whilst I was always a good pianist. I did enjoy this experience of playing for my friends. I have often played at Stansted since then, but that is the occasion which remains in my memory.

It was such a good day! John Biggin and Joan Bornstein — both concert pianists — played while Jean Buck, a well known BBC and opera singer, sang. I can't remember now what they played, but everyone enjoyed themselves. There were 500 visitors, and we were all very busy making sure all went well.

Sometimes, in the beginning we would meet, just a small

group. We made our own meals and achieved so much. There was a marvellous kitchen garden which helped supply the vegetables for guests. That had to be discontinued in the end because the cost of production outweighed the produce.

I often look back now as I see the almost constant stream of people in the college. Most of them are students, but some do come just to enjoy the wonderful spiritual atmosphere. I know we were right in holding on to the hall, a centre of spirituality now known right around the world.

To sell Stansted would have meant the end of our money problems, but been a devastating action which I believe would have repercussions throughout our movement. Money goes. It is spent. Then what heritage would we hand on to those who follow us?

How would we face the spirit world and admit we had sold an ideal, a dream? How would we face all those thousands who have put their trust in Spirit, their work, their effort and their money into Stansted to perpetuate that dream?

I receive so many letters from people. Some cannot even speak our language. They tell me how their time at Stansted has meant so much to them, what they have learnt and how their visit has changed their very lives. They take their experience back to their own homes, often into countries where they do not have access even to Spiritualist churches let alone a centre such as the Arthur Findlay College.

We have had so many jolly times at Stansted. Working together creates a bond. When you return again and again to the same place to work you see old friends. I like that.

I remember my first Dinner Dance there as the president of both the Friends of Stansted and the union. Mother was present in fine form along with so many friends. Maurice Barbanell, my old friend and protagonist from "Psychic News," was guest of honour. I was able to hand over £2,000 from the Friends to reduce our debt just that little bit more.

Grace Boyers was also there. She was one of the first, in fact I think she was the first trustee, of Stansted. Tom Johanson, former general secretary of the Spiritualist Association of Great Britain, gave a witty speech and managed to promote the newly formed

Council of Spiritualists, which we had formed between the union, the SAGB, the Greater World League and the Union — now the Institute — of Spiritualist Mediums. The council was not to last too long, but the idea was good.

We should co-operate. Even though we don't all believe exactly the same way, we do all believe in Spiritualism. This is the wonder of Stansted. It is run by the union, but all are welcome. Unity was the theme of my talk that night. It often was, often is and, I trust, will always be my aim.

The year that central heating was extended to the upper floors was a landmark. It meant we could extend the time the college was open to the public. I cannot talk about Stansted and leave out my old friends Christene and Roy Wandless. For more years than I care to remember they have helped and supported the work done at the hall. There have been years when we would have been hard pressed but for their generosity of spirit. They are both friends of mine and have supported me in my spiritual work.

There have been so many, some now passed, who gave freely of time, effort and money. It is too easy to view things from the position we are now in and to forget where we were and where we would have been without the love of those who have cared. We must never forget Spiritualists and friends, such as Eva French, who have raised many thousands of pounds for Stansted Hall.

Now, it has become my dream to have a healing clinic centred at Stansted Hall. I believe that spiritual healing is going to be more and more important. I do not think we have paid enough attention to this over the years.

I have always encouraged the various "weeks" held at the hall to have regular healing services included in their programmes. I think this is such an important part of our work. It was in the Sanctuary at Stansted that the first meeting of the committee of the Guild of Spiritualist Healers was held.

In 1975 I heard of some apparently marvellous work being done in the Philippines by a medium healer called Juan Blanche. It involved what is known as psychic surgery. The medium is able to open the body without using instruments and effectively give healing through this method.

I felt it was important we should at least look at this type of healing and arranged for Mr Blanche to visit us at Stansted. Indeed, I felt so strongly about this that I personally guaranteed to underwrite the cost of his visit.

Afterwards, I was going to arrange a special healing conference which would cover all the aspects of healing, not just this special method. I felt really excited and enthusiastic.

We anticipated that 200 a day would visit during the time Juan Blanche was to be with us. All sorts of arrangements had been made to cope with this influx. We had extra staff, marquees, sound equipment and even mirrors so that the operations could be fully observed.

I received a cable from Hong Kong saying that Mr Blanche was on his way. Mother was to come with me to Stansted, but she changed her mind. I asked her why because I knew she wanted to see this man work.

"He will not get there, Gordon," she said. "Frank has been to see me. He told me there is no need to go to Stansted because Blanche has not left Manila." My good friend Frank, who had passed on the previous year, was always very close to Mother. I thought she was not right, but I did not argue and left her at home.

I told some people about this when I got to Stansted rather jokingly really for we had got everything ready for this visit. People were there from all over the country. I was not prepared to believe that all had been for nothing! I also wanted to have healing for my voice. I had been involved in a car accident and was speaking in a rather irritating whisper. I was quite convinced Mother was wrong, but should have known better!

When Mr Blanche didn't turn up we went mad. We couldn't even find out at first where he was. I received a cable from him and was so worried. I felt responsible for him, for all the many people who travelled to receive healing and for the arrangements which had been made. I felt quite ill!

I felt I was responsible because I had pushed for it to take place. Thank goodness, at least, there had been no accident. Mr Blanche had been unable to get a clearance for his visa and, as Mother had said, never even left Manila.

I did arrange for some people to have healing before they left the hall. One of them was Gwen Williams from Bangor in Wales.

I saw her in the Sanctuary and took her hand. Her daughter was there. So was Peter Williams, a friend of mine.

The guides came in very quickly, with Paddy introducing himself. He gave Gwen a complete diagnosis of her problems. Then Peter gave her healing. I know this helped her because she felt immediate improvement.

The nice part was that while Paddy was talking, my voice returned to its full power. Unfortunately, it went right back to being just a whisper as I came out of the trance. It didn't occur to me at the time to ask for my own healing!

I was determined we should have the opportunity of watching the methods used by these Filipino healers, but it was to be another three years before we could arrange this.

At last, in 1978 I was able to get David and Helen Elizalde to visit England and demonstrate at Stansted. These two young people were quite charming and very gifted.

Helen lived in Australia where she was married to a successful doctor and working as a beautician. She heard a voice which asked her to leave all she had and go to the Philippines to work for the poor in that country.

Helen did not hesitate, but her husband did not feel able to abandon everything he had worked for in Australia on the instructions of a "voice" so they parted. Helen was so sure this was what she must do and had the courage of her conviction. It was in the Philippines that she met David — and at once recognised that he was the one with whom she would work.

He, too, had undergone a similar experience and been drawn to expand his gift of healing. They started a clinic in a house which was given to them by a grateful patient. Here they attended to all those who needed their help. They turned no-one away and took only what was offered.

Too often this was nothing. Eventually, they had to return to Australia to continue their work. The sheer poverty in the Philippines defeated their good intentions. They were starving and could not support David's brothers and sisters, who were dependent upon them.

It might seem to be a dramatic story, but, told to me in the Blue Room at Stansted where so many "wonders" have been enacted, I did not doubt it for a moment.

Helen and David are linked spiritually when they work together, both hearing a "voice like thunder" directing them. They hear this voice simultaneously, although it is not audible to others who are there. They do work separately at times. When they were at Stansted, the couple worked in the cubicles in the Sanctuary, sometimes in separate cubicles, other times side by side.

Many accusations have been made about the work that they did in England. The most emotive was that they were charging patients and making a lot of money. I would like to say now that they did not charge. David and Helen were paid all their expenses, and given a decent donation for their time and trouble.

I think that is fair. Patients were asked for only £10. This covered two consultations, plus an operation if one was thought to be required. No guarantees were given. Many successes were reported both in 1978 and the following year, including myself.

Yes, I decided that I, too, would like to benefit from this healing. Many people know that I have suffered with my health for a number of years. At that time my legs were very swollen. The local doctor said it was excess fluid and, of course, I have been plagued with phlebitis.

David diagnosed too much sugar in my body — which was actually quite right — and then they operated...on my chest! There were about 80 people watching. I am sure they wondered what was happening for most of them knew I was troubled in my lower half. What neither they nor the Elizaldes knew was that for some time I had been suffering the most excruciating pains in the chest.

I had had X-rays, which showed scar tissue on my lungs. I suffered breathlessness and dizzy spells — and really felt much better after the operation. The peculiar part is that my leg cleared up most wonderfully well. It was quite marvellous. Neither David nor Helen had gone near my legs, but they started to clear by the very next day.

The two people from BBC TV's "Nationwide" team were invited to watch. This was no hole in the corner affair. Later it transpired someone had secreted blood in a handkerchief, and stated that analysis showed it to be not of human origin, but "close to" the pig family.

It is odd that the blood I had analysed was considered to be human — and that which another person said they had examined from a bowl was said to react as though it were from the pig family. The blood came from the same source: me!

I cannot believe this. It is not as though there was anywhere to store vast quantities of either human or animal blood at Stansted, certainly not where the team was working. There are stone walls in the Sanctuary. Only a thin curtain separated the cubicles.

The place was not secured when the Elizaldes were not working. People were wandering in and out at various times to witness what was happening. The curtains were, at most times, kept open.

We allowed "Nationwide" cameras and reporters in to film the events. Yet they did not convey the full information when the programme was broadcast. I think they were unfair in this.

Magicians were brought in, claiming that the blood was concealed in little balloons held under the fingers as David or Helen operated. What nonsense. Where would they have got little balloons?

I have this vision of the staff at Stansted sitting around the kitchen table, a teaspoon in one hand, a piece of rubber in the other and a big bowl of congealing blood in front of them saying, "Please don't bring these people here again, Mr. Higginson."

Not a nice thought, is it? Well, that is what the magician was suggesting in effect. That we supplied these balloons, stored them and then disposed of the empties afterwards. They didn't suggest how this could be done in front of so many witnesses or how we kept everyone quiet.

Goodness, I did get so cross when I read the papers and saw all these things on television. So much good had been done, so many people had been helped. Not everyone was cured. But that was never promised.

It is so easy to be negative about things that are not usual, not understood. I do not know if this type of healing is right for Britain, but I do know we have a duty to look at these things.

We followed up on quite a few of the patients and found that some benefited in the long term, others for a shorter time. I don't think this is important. There is often an underlying cause for illness. If the cause is not treated, the effect may re-occur. In all the treatments at Stansted people were asked to follow through by having healing from their local church.

We were unable to have further visits from the Elizaldes. The comments which had been made culminated in a complaint being made. We were never able to answer this complaint. Indeed, we did not hear about it directly but through the national papers.

When we made enquiries we were told that if the Elizaldes returned they might be held for questioning about a complaint that was made the previous year. It was very vague, but we would not wish to subject two dedicated workers to such indignity.

This type of work opens up a new — or is it an old? — vista of healing. I have said I am not sure that it is right for England. It does not conform to spiritual healing as the Guild of Spiritualist Healers — which is part of the union — defines it.

I want to open out the healing at Stansted. I would, ideally, like to open a proper hospital or clinic in the grounds. I think we should have all sorts of therapies available. I know this is ambitious, but truly believe there is a place for this in our movement.

I am sure that spiritual healing and its allied therapies holds much for the future. We should also be looking at preventative therapies, diagnosis of potential areas of imbalance and finding answers.

Recently, over the past two years I have reinstated a project which I introduced some years ago at Stansted — special healing weeks. People can come to these as residents and receive all kinds of help. They also have the support of people who understand around them.

I am also looking at the possibility of having a clinic where people would have access to various types of complementary therapies, such as aromatherapy, acupuncture and reflexology. These would be booked in advance. We would have a list of specialists to call upon when necessary.

This would be the value of an established clinic. We would find out which was the best form of treatment for an individual and then, if necessary, bring in someone who specialised in that treatment.

I believe that Stansted is the ideal place for such a centre. If it were successful, we could branch out into the main areas of Britain. In Brazil, there are special hospitals where this sort of treatment is available. Why not in Britain?

Looking to training for the future, many times I have stated both in meetings and in interviews for papers that I think we should be making more effort to train our young mediums. I have talked this over with the chairpersons of both our Education and Exponents Committees. These are two very able people, Vi Kipling and Rose Thompson.

They have done sterling work changing and updating the syllabus for students and methods of assessing our workers, which is becoming very professional. I think we need this, although I shall keep a watchful eye open for I do not think we should lose sight of the spirituality involved in our work. For if we were to lose this, we have lost that which is vital to Spiritualism and would be treading the slippery slope of Orthodoxy.

It is difficult sometimes to keep the balance. We must move towards a proper college status for Stansted. This requires a professional approach, but some of our best workers are not academically minded and we must not lose these. They have given too much to Spiritualism to leave behind just because they don't like to take exams.

I have had to give up running some of the weeks that I did enjoy. Simplicity and Awareness are two of these. They are the starter courses. My dear friend, medium Mavis Pattilla, has taken them over. I have asked that we should have more advanced courses so those who have been through the beginner's weeks can move forward.

I have handed these basic weeks over, although I do still take part of the week so I can concentrate on other weeks where the training is more intense. I did start to call these "Advanced Weeks" but people got the wrong idea.

I am very aware that very few people can afford more than one or at most two weeks a year and so had this idea. We should have weeks where we can have different levels of instruction, one moving forward from where the other left off. I think that until the time comes when we can subsidise students to come and take a full time course of study, this is the best way.

I do have a fund which I use to pay for certain young mediums who need the further training and experience that Stansted can give. I actually put any donations churches give me for my work straight into this fund.

One day I visualise serious students coming for six months or a year so we can take them in hand. Then they will go out to the districts and the world properly trained.

I know this is in advance of what we can do at present, but we must have the courage to think ahead — of what we should be doing rather than what we can do. I have always believed that Spirit will help us to help ourselves.

Chapter 16

GETTING GOOD EVIDENCE

TRAINING is so important to all who are going to work for the spirit world — and I cannot emphasise this enough. Over all these years I have declared in public that we do not pay sufficient attention to getting ourselves ready, looking at our young mediums and making sure they have a good knowledge.

So many have not been taught properly. That is why I have asked that there should be a good teachers' training course. There must be more people who can teach others, but they must know how to do it properly. Our future is in the hands of those who are just starting out. And all too often they don't even know what good evidence is.

This is a subject which should be taught to all potential mediums as they start, perhaps even before they begin their training. Too many mediums seen upon the platform do not make enough effort, do not even know what is good proof of survival and do not know when they are not giving even the basics of evidence!

I was fortunate when I was young because I first had my mother to make sure that I made the effort and had a good training. Then I met with so many really good mediums. It is important for a potential medium to look to see how other people work.

This is not to copy how they work, but to observe, to see that the evidence being presented is obtained from the spirit world, to notice that they take time to get to know their spirit communicator and finally to understand that they must work for the love of spirit with humility and yet a certainty that comes with knowing you have made strong the bridge between the worlds.

I remember when I took a meeting and Ernest Thompson was

to be the speaker. I was a very nice young man in those days, slim, good looking and very smart. I have always liked nice clothes and always tried to look smart. I also had the confidence of spirit mixed in with the uncertainty of youth.

I arrived. Ernest Thompson, one of the really great people in Spiritualism, said to me, "Now Gordon, I want you to demonstrate first." "Oh, I can't do that," I replied. "Yes you can," he said.

Well, I never demonstrated first: I always waited for the speaker to pave the way and then come in the glory. Ernest insisted so I asked "Why?" But he wouldn't tell me, just that that was the way he wanted it. So I said "Yes," thinking to myself, "I shall tell my mother when I get back home." I was only about 16 at the time, very young, and told Mother everything in those days!

I demonstrated and sat down, expecting a hymn to be sung before he gave the address. No, there was no hymn. Ernest asked all the people who had received messages to stand up. It so happened I thought I had been really marvellous that night and so was not too worried at first.

He questioned all the recipients concerning the contents of their messages in great detail. Ernest had taken it all down in shorthand. He picked out one lady in particular. I had brought back her husband and given good evidence, so I thought. So did she.

After Ernest went through the things I had given, he stated it was quite good, but did not constitute good evidence. I thought "Who does he think he is!" I was very young and quite full of myself as youngsters are. I always give evidence in my demonstrations.

Then Ernest pointed out that evidence is not always what people know, but what they don't know. He went on to say that this lady had three, perhaps four, times said "No" where she wasn't sure. He asked her whether she could check up on these things. The recipient replied she could try. Mr Thompson asked her to go out there and then and telephone around to see whether these facts could be verified.

I was amazed. No-one, apart from my mother, had ever queried my work like this. He continued the meeting. And when the lady came back, she was able to report that I had been quite right.

Ernest was demonstrating — and extremely well — that we must be wary of how much comes from the consciousness of the recipient and how much comes from the spirit world. I have always been aware of this and try to remember the lesson he taught me that day.

The evidence of survival can be in the "No" rather than in the "Yes!" The very fact that we have an inner power must be taken into account. As mediums we should be able to tell you more than you, the recipient, know; we should be able to show that Spirit have knowledge of things that have happened since they left the earth plane.

We must prove not only that entities have existed on earth, but that they continue to exist in Spirit and increased their knowledge since they went there. We must show that their memories and minds are still functioning.

This is called the "bridging of the gap." If a child has passed and is contacted, he or she should be aware of other things within the family; the passing of another member, the birth of another child. This is proving intelligent survival, an on-going existence.

There are always spiritual influences around us. But until we are consciously aware and make effort to contact and use those spiritual powers, we can't really get the help which is offered.

Once we begin to go into development, not to develop one specific gift, but to expand the powers which are spiritual which help our minds make that link with the spiritual influences around us, we become aware.

It is that which changes our lives around us. I have always said that I think potential mediums should spend time in learning about their own spirit before trying to make links with other spirits. We have a conscious, a subconscious and a superconscious mind. All three play their part in the giving of a message.

It is from the superconscious mind we get those spiritual influences. If this does not happen, then there is no point to life. Mediumship comes from the subconsciousness, for that is where the work is involved.

Let us think of the knowledge that came through the influence of the guides and spirits around people like Andrew Jackson Davis or Emma Hardinge Britten, neither of whom had a great deal of education. Indeed, Andrew Jackson Davis had very little earthly education.

These people had contact with their superconscious state and were able to bring forward the most wonderful understanding. They filled halls where thousands of people gathered to listen to them speaking on a diversity of subjects. They wrote books and demonstrated the continuity of life.

From the guiding force within and the spirit influence around them, their superstate was filled with a knowledge that was contained within their subconscious from where they were able to bring it forward into their conscious mind and share it with other people. Mediums like this could talk on virtually every subject asked of them.

Any trance medium will tell you that when we hear anything of ourself when working there will be times when we say, "Well, I can't accept that." Then we find that six months later it has become part of our own belief and we accept it as a fact because at the point of when it came into consciousness it was more knowledge than we could accept. We were not yet ready for it, but the guides know that this is a point where we must go forward and extend the knowledge we have.

The mind has changed because the influence of the spirit world has remained in the subconscious and eventually becomes a part of experience. It's like reading a book.

I remember Meurig Morris, the great medium, who said to her guide one day she was fed up with all this information coming through, much of which she didn't even believe, and all of which she didn't know where it was coming from. Meurig wanted to know who her guide, Power, was, and who was in her body while she was working.

One day she heard the guide speak to her as she was coming out of the trance state. "Meurig," he said. "Look to your right and see for yourself who is in your body when you are in the state of trance." She did so — and saw herself!

The guide, or spirit, does not enter your body, but only merges with your superstate. Only you inhabit your body. The more you develop that superstate, the more easily Spirit can blend with you. That is what development is all about. It isn't about deciding what sort of medium you want to be: it is about developing the knowledge of your consciousness to make yourself available without dictating to Spirit what you want.

There is such a lot of nonsense talked about development. For instance, some people say you must not sit on your own. They are obviously worried there is an evil spirit waiting to get at you.

How do you think those first mediums developed? They didn't know all these things — and didn't go mad. They were chosen instruments of Spirit, chosen because they were gifted. They had wonderful spiritual experiences which led them into the work. They were chosen to serve God and the spirit world.

I do, however, think that circle work can play an important role in development, but it should be led by a teacher, someone who knows and can guide mediums to achieve their potential.

The psychic development will come to the student first, then the sensitivity will develop and then on to spirit links. If there is no-one to tell you that you have not developed sufficiently well, everyone is accepting the lesser link and you feel successful: you may never improve.

There are now a number of working mediums who have realised they have not been trained properly and seek further help and advice.

A basic rule should be that you can identify the spirit communicator. You ought to be given sufficient evidence of their identity to be sure that you are linking the right people together. Do not be satisfied with less.

Memories of when they were on the earth can help to pin down the right recipient, but there must be more. Have they exhibited personality, character and feelings? Can they prove to satisfaction that they have added to the sum total of their experience since they went into Spirit?

Have they met people from the same family who passed since they went? Have they observed events in the family? Have they extra knowledge? Can they give the recipient some information which is not known at the time of the sitting, but has to be checked? This latter is ideal, but cannot be used on its own. It must be given together with identity and other evidence.

I can just imagine dozens of mediums travelling around the

Why, it seems only yesterday this photo was taken, but it was, in fact, during the dark days of the last world war. Here I am with two friends in Greece. The young lady, a gifted pianist, attended an astonishing materialisation seance with me.

I'm not sure how old I was when this photo was taken, but think it was probably during my early twenties. Oh, if only I'd dated my photographs!

Happy days at a Christmas Fayre. Here I am with my sister Hazel (extreme right) and business partner Frank Tams, one of my closest friends.

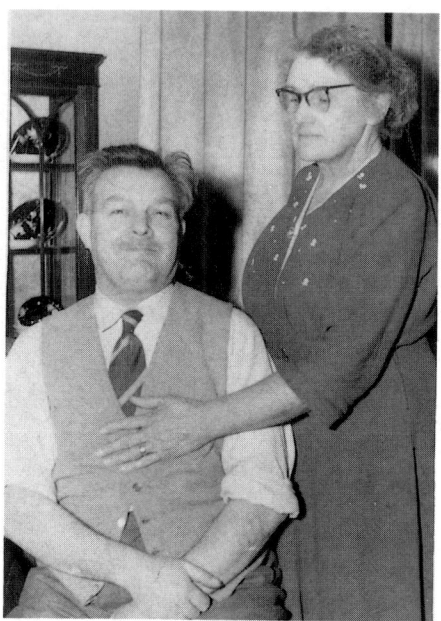

Mother meant the world to me . . . and still does. It was she who taught me the basics of mediumship — and only the best would do! This is one of the few photos of her wearing glasses. And, as you will read, a pair of spectacles helped to prove her survival.

I don't know why, but I look a little sheepish here. My brother Arthur certainly seems pleased with himself.

I was not always portly, you know! Here is a slim young me talking with some fellow Spiritualists as medium Ena Twigg looks on. I think this photo must have been taken in the 1940s or thereabouts.

Jean, a young girl bed-bound with arthritis and TB, was given healing by us, but I knew she would pass. Later she returned at a materialisation seance, full of life and fighting fit.

Here is Arthur Findlay – and I feel so very privileged to have helped turn his dream of a Spiritualist College into a reality.

There are countless friends' photographs I could include if space would allow, but I chose this one of Eric Hatton since one day when the hour comes he will succeed me as President of the Spiritualists' National Union. He and his wife, Heather — pictured at a "Psychic News" dinner dance — helped to nurse me back to full health after I suffered several strokes. I love them both dearly.

Of all the places I love, the Arthur Findlay College comes right at the top. Here is just one view of the college, which I am proud to say attracts Spiritualists from all over the world. For me, it's a second home, one where I not only teach but meet friends old and new.

circuit and saying: "I have your grandfather here. He says your mother was ill just before you were born. You don't know that now, but that is all right because Gordon Higginson has said that the best evidence is that which you don't know. You must go away and check this."

After a year, for example, if the medium returns to a church, no-one can remember what they had to check or whether it was right. No, that will not do at all! There must be reasonable proof given or everyone will wonder what on earth you are up to and they won't think it is spirit communication at all.

You must take time to know who you are working with. They may not necessarily give a name, although they will allow you to give a name for your own comfort. They must become your closest friend. Without my friends from the spirit world where would I have been all these years? I have had the intimate closeness of Spirit in a way that few have experienced in their lives; I have known their intervention both in my training and in my life.

All these things have taken their price. When a person devotes as much time as I have to a life of travel and dedication, they must make sacrifices.

Chapter 17

TO UNITE ALL PEOPLES

I HAVE said it was the attitude and help that the SNU gave to my own church that led me first to think favourably of the organisation as a whole. I was also impressed because without the union the Fraudulent Mediums Act would never have been passed and we, as mediums, would not have the freedom we now have to work and worship in the way that seems right to us.

I think there are still many people who are now as I was then, aware of the union — members even, through their own church or Class 'B' membership — but not yet aware of how important their membership is. I came to this realisation through what could be termed personal gain. Any benefit to my church was as if it were my own!

I have thought a lot about this. It was part of the reason I decided to have a Publicity Committee so that we had someone whose job it was to take notice of these things — to bring a closeness and greater understanding between the members and those who run the organisation.

It is easy to be over-awed and to think of those in positions of authority as being different from yourself, but it is a fact that all these were ordinary church members at one time or the other. True, they have to join in as Class 'B' members before they can take position outside their own church, but everyone starts as rank and file. I was — and look where I am!

When I was young, there were so many great people who seemed to be special. I could write a whole book about them, but instead I have picked just a few whom I humbly feel free to have called my friend. They had started as we all do — as ordinary but committed members.

I knew John Stewart and will always count it a privilege that I did so. It was he who spearheaded the campaign to get our Bill passed, he who persuaded MPs to help us even though they were not Spiritualists. Indeed the man who finally presented the Bill was a Methodist!

Once John had the most wonderful acknowledgement of his efforts from the world of spirit. It was at a meeting in Glasgow with medium Tom Tyrell. James Robertson, the Grand Old Man of Scottish Spiritualism, was chairing. John was in the audience. Tom described how he saw Spirit take a mantle from around James' shoulders and place it upon the shoulders of John.

John wore that mantle well for James passed soon after this and John was called upon to succeed him as the President of the Glasgow Association of Spiritualists, the largest SNU church in the country. John later filled the offices of president, vice-president and treasurer of the union as well as the president of the London District Council, which was the largest district in the country.

John was a marvellous example of someone who devoted his life to Spiritualism. He gave his energies in his own area, but had the vision to recognise that the local church or society is linked into the national organisation, managing to serve both without depriving either.

It is very easy to be parochial when you are concerned only with one church. There are always so many worries attached to the running of a church that one's view can become limited within that one small area.

It was, however, the dream of Arthur Findlay that finally led me to the recognition that without the union, Spiritualism would remain just a collection of individual churches each going their own way, having no collective goal. If the dream of our pioneers was to become reality, then we must pull together.

If we were to be a world wide organisation to unite all peoples — and I truly believe that this is the aim of Spirit in this venture — we not only needed a centre such as Stansted, but a strong organisation to follow the directions of the spirit world. This organisation would have to become a strength to be listened to.

Thanks to my contacts with good mediums and wonderful workers, I had many friends within the union so I started to attend national meetings. I had been invited to become a minister and was very happy to accept this great responsibility.

I should say here that I came to the conclusion it was then far too easy to become a minister. When I eventually became the president, I introduced new qualifications.

I had not thought that so much of my subsequent career would be concerned with the SNU. My mother certainly did not want this. She belonged to a union church and was loyal, but never thought as much about the organisation as I did. Mother did not see happiness for me in that direction, but once you have truly accepted Spirit in your life as I had, you also accept their direction.

In 1963, I went to the union's Worthing conference. It was such a noisy meeting, with so many different opinions being expressed. I was annoyed because the council had sold our shares in "Psychic News." There were arguments about the make-up of the council. It was proposed that a committee should be appointed to look into this.

I look back and sometimes regret the passing of some of our more vociferous characters, but not entirely. There were some terrible meetings in the past when one would get up and then another and tempers would rise. I see this happening now, but do wish people would say what they need to in a reasonable manner as sometimes tempers do get heated.

In the end, at Worthing, a solution was reached. A six-man advisory committee was set up to consider how to resolve the solvency of the union, and to consider the efficiency and composition of the council with a view to change. I was asked to sit on this committee. The others were Laurence Wilson, then of Manchester, Dr J. Malcolm of Glasgow, Harold Vigurs, a former president, Norman Ainley from South Shields and Wilfred Watts of London.

Members wanted people who were not on the council so they could take a dispassionate look and assess the situation. It was really from this committee that my ideas for the new system of organisation were formed. I introduced these in the 1970s at Swanwick. It is known as the Three Tier System.

Just after conference that year, I was taken ill with a bad attack of shingles. It was not the shock of being asked to work at national level, but the result of overwork. I had suffered a number of worries and was travelling hundreds of miles to meetings. But all these problems seem quite minor in retrospect.

I was asked to be a governor of the Arthur Findlay College. This pleased me, although the task before us was frightening. We had to turn around a monstrous debt in as short a time as possible. I believed whole-heartedly in the future of the college, but there were so many who wanted just to give up, sell and cut our losses.

I gave a sitting to Arthur Findlay before his passing and had a long conversation with him about his plans, his dreams, for Stansted. I knew what he wanted: it was not to sell what would be the birthright of our future generations.

It was in 1969 that I became vice-president of the union. Believe me, I still only considered my position at national level a temporary position. This was not the job I wanted to do in life. I was a medium. My task was to prove survival, not to direct the members of my religion in things that seemingly had little to do with Spirit.

The following year changed my future and my life. I think that I came into the time that Spirit had prepared me for during all these years. I had been trained well as a medium; I had taken training in business management; I had come through difficulties and still liked helping people, although I admit that my trust in them was not as naive as it had been.

I was in a very fortunate position because I had bought into a business where my partner was a very good friend and also a dedicated Spiritualist. I was able to take far more time off than the average man who had to earn a living.

When I was asked to take the position as president, I refused the nomination. It would be just too much. The union faced virtual bankruptcy. I suppose I didn't want to be the president when this happened.

Spirit decided otherwise. They sent a messenger to me and asked me to reconsider my refusal. There was no pressure, just a gentle confrontation. My refusal would be understood and never judged. No man is forced into his destiny. It has to be a free decision. Mine was made, perhaps before I was even born!

Once I had accepted the position of the president, it meant I had to go to many different places and meet with many different people. I have been privileged to meet with many great people.

These could not help but have influence upon my life.

Harold Vigurs, a great man, was already a good friend. He had a fine legal mind and a tremendous knowledge of Spiritualism. We became more like father and son. Harold gave me tremendous help and spiritual guidance both with the union and with my personal affairs. It was he who was responsible for organising a Belgium tour, which I undertook in 1953.

I had seldom worked abroad, but found I did enjoy the experience. I know that basically the work was the same, but there was somehow a feeling of festivity just by virtue of the fact that one was in such different surroundings.

I have to say I have had many opportunities offered to me to work overseas, but there has been so very much to do in this country for the union. It was my decision to devote my life in this way, but I was very much influenced by the dear friends I have in the spirit world.

One place I have worked abroad since I became president was in 1980 when I went to Gibraltar. The first time I went there was only a three-day visit, a wonderful experience. I do like gracious living — and this was a taste of very gracious living indeed!

Ray Smith, the President of the Gibraltar Psychic Research Society, was my host. I stayed on his yacht and was taken to and from the hall where I worked. At the end of my final demonstration everyone just stood up and clapped. Of course, I had been superb! Really, I worked very well.

I especially remember one contact made. It was the mother of a Carmen Anthony. I described her daughter's house and even gave her address in full. Her mother so wanted Carmen to know that she visited her and knew all about her activities; she even told me about a plant which had just flowered.

It was a moving moment for Carmen. She told me afterwards I had mentioned her mother's Cameo broach, which had always been special but would mean even more to her now. Carmen said she really needed that contact.

I gave foreign names and addresses just as I had so many years ago when I worked with Harold in Bruges. The gift never fades, does it? One man came up to me afterwards. He had been so determined to see me work that he went to his Bishop and obtained special permission to attend!

Many queued. In fact, there was a line of people a quarter of a mile long. Only the first 700 got in. I enjoyed my visit, but accepted few invitations of that nature. Duty to the union and a growing involvement in organisation meant I could very seldom get away even if I had wanted to. My life had set into a pattern which is, even now, the centre of my existence.

Chapter 18

SEEING THE DEAD

I HAVE had many friends over the years. A lot were made through my work and have remained a working relationship, but a few seemed to be something more. I have worked with some of the best mediums in the world and witnessed so many wonders that I sometimes feel very humble.

I do not think there is anyone left alive who has worked in so many places, churches, centres, halls — both large and small — in this country. I never turned down a meeting just because there would be few there in number, but was always aware I was working first for the spirit world. If I could change the meaning of life for just one person at a meeting then I had fulfilled the task for which I was both chosen and trained.

I believe I have worked with more of the great mediums than any other person in this century, and know for certain that I am the only one left from those days still working except for Ursula Roberts who was, and still is, a really marvellous worker for the spirit world. Ursula went on to do more teaching and healing. Her guide, Ramadahn, has a wonderful way of putting things. Others that come to mind are that great clairvoyant Billy Redmond who passed on to his higher reward a few years ago, and Ivy Northage.

I think the last time I worked with Billy was at the Royal Albert Hall, where he was booked as the speaker. He did very well, although being a brilliant clairvoyant, was always a better demonstrator than a speaker. Through the many great mediums with whom I have worked over these years I have had many really wonderful experiences.

I remember one time when I had taken a large meeting in the

City Hall, Newcastle on Tyne. The speaker that night was Hunter Selkirk whilst my old friend Gladys Mallaburn, who had arranged the event, was demonstrating with me.

The meeting was packed and very successful. People had to be turned away. They could not find room for all those who wanted to attend. Afterwards, Gladys and I were invited back to Hunter Selkirk's home.

He had a very humble home. Hunter was a coal miner; his house was not large, but very homely, and filled with love. There he gave us a materialisation seance which I shall never forget.

I saw a girl sitting upon his knee. She was one of his guides, and had such a beautiful face. An aunt of mine, Emily, came and spoke to me, giving some very good evidence. I enjoyed that because I was always very close to my family so it was wonderful to see her again and be able to speak with her.

An old friend of mine, who I knew in the war, built up quite well. It was George. He took hold of my hand. I felt his so very clearly. Hunter had a hard hand, a little rough if anything. But George had a soft hand...and the difference was marked. I checked afterwards and asked Hunter if I could feel his hand. It was marvellous to talk again to my old friend. I felt so humble in the face of such mediumship.

There were so many great materialisation mediums. I took a meeting in Cardiff and was asked afterwards with Mabel Hibbs and Captain Williams to the home of Alec Harris. We were invited to sit in on an impromptu seance with him. His wife and a circle of his friends sat with us.

One thing struck me about this particular seance. I did not have a personal contact during it, but was impressed by the remarkable difference between Harris and his guide, an Indian Brave. I was invited to stand and feel the materialised body of this guide, and was struck by the texture of the skin and the feel of muscle beneath the flesh.

At one point we were instructed to pull the curtains back — and could not see the body of the medium. A knock came upon the door of the room...and Alec Harris was outside! We let him in. Of course, the sceptic would find his absence from the cabinet good reason for doubt. They would probably say he had physically left the room by another way to re-enter through the door.

They would not take into account the circumstances of this ordinary house, which precluded any such action, or the integrity of this wonderful medium who did not need to stoop to trickery. For them, the sceptics, this fantastic power is not recognised. There is no power known to science which can match that which is of the universe.

When you come to understand that, the seance-room proves it to you. When you have experienced that, there is no further need for any proof. You begin to recognise, in a way that is unique, that there is a purpose to our lives.

One of the most moving seances I experienced was with an old lady in Greece during the war. At this seance I saw my own guide, Cuckoo, move forward into the centre of the room. She sat on my knee, something she has done many times when I have been entranced, but here I was able to feel her, kiss her and feel her kiss me. It was so very moving.

During that seance a friend of mine who had been killed in the war came back. He appeared and spoke to me in English. The medium could speak no English whatsoever. She was a wonderful lady, someone I shall never forget.

Many mediums in other countries work in the background because Spiritualism is not known or accepted in their land. We are so lucky here in this country. We now have this liberty and some of the finest mediums in the world.

We have good mediums now, but not as they were in the past. I have worked with those who were really great. Only a few remember many of these, people like Estelle Roberts, Helen Hughes, Estelle Stead, Susy Hughes, Stella Hughes, Armand Wilson and Jordan Gill. These mediums were of the highest calibre. They dedicated their lives to bringing comfort to thousands. These I have called my friends. I think I am the only one left who has worked with all these great names from the past. There was Magdalene Kelly, Ena Twigg and Jean Thompson, who helped me tremendously.

I remember working with a medium called Penny Hardwick. Her name was Elsie, but people called her Penny after she got stuck in one of these toilets where you had to put a penny in the slot to open the door. Her friends called to her through the door with instructions, but nothing would work. She couldn't open the door from the inside so they had to go away to find another penny!

Penny came to my home. Whilst not young then, she always looked smart. Penny was a heavy smoker and quite a heavy drinker, who loved a stout.

On one occasion at my home she had several glasses of her favourite beverage and said to Mother, "Fanny, I am going to give you a sitting." "Oh, no," said Mother, thinking to herself that Penny was not quite herself.

"Yes," said Penny. "There is someone here who wants to talk to you." I asked if I could sit in on this. It was agreed that I should. Mrs Hardwick went into trance. Now, my mother was a wonderful woman and had seen and talked to my father many times since he passed.

Mother and father had a good relationship without it being an over-loving one. They had respect and a friendship for each other. It worked very well. We had been a close and happy family.

My father's voice came through the medium, giving so many items of family detail which Mrs Hardwick could not possibly have known. Mother and I were very moved. She gave us such very good evidence of his survival and his continued love for us.

He turned to speak to me, giving the name of Mons. This was an abbreviation of my middle name, which my father had insisted upon. He had been at the Battle of Mons and was one of those who saw the Angel of Mons. My name was in remembrance of this wonderful incident in his life.

Then she spoke of my brother Arthur as Gordon. Now Arthur had never liked his name. When he went to work on the Isle of White — he was in the prison service and married one of the officer's daughters there — he insisted on being called Gordon, which he had always liked.

This could be quite complicated when we were all together and so they called me Mons, as my father did. No one outside the family could know this. And no-one else had called me by this name.

Penny was an excellent medium. I have often thought of this sitting. Father and I were not as close as I was to Mother, but we loved each other very much. I thought of this incident when choosing a title for this book.

There were many mediums who played an important part in the 1970s when I became president of the union, but two who stand out in my memory were Maurice Barbanell and Harry Edwards.

The union was in financial difficulties so I appealed to these, together with some other famous mediums for help. I thought that if we had a publicity campaign throughout the country, we could raise the money which was so desperately needed.

In all the times I worked and shared the platform with them, I do not remember them ever asking for a penny. Harry never stated a fee. He never did, not even at his sanctuary at Shere, Surrey. He would accept a retiring collection, but never did he demand a penny for his services.

Harry started the National Federation of Spiritual Healers, with which I didn't agree. I always thought we should stick together, but the union was not quite ready for his ideas. Each person must follow their own destiny. Harry did so. And he was right to do so.

His sanctuary is still world famous, the work being continued by his chosen successors, Ray and Joan Branch. We have continued on friendly terms for I do believe in co-operation wherever possible.

Just before, during and after the war there were a lot of meetings in the London area. You could go to these large halls on Saturday and Sunday and see really good mediums.

Estelle Roberts would demonstrate at the Aeolian Hall whilst Meurig Morris took a theatre. Jo Benjamin hired Alliance Hall, and Robert Strong another one, but I can't remember the name just now. So many halls were in use — the Queens Hall, the Victoria Hall, and all packed to capacity.

Meurig Morris came to the Potteries one year at the invitation of my mother. The Jubilee Hall in Stoke Town Hall was booked: it held about six hundred. Meurig — or rather Power, her guide — was to give a trance address; no-one ever gave clairvoyance after one of her demonstrations. She was a very smart lady, always well groomed, wearing beautiful long dresses.

Meurig had a very nice feminine voice. She would sit there

quietly, always looking very much the lady, then standing, without a microphone, start to speak. Giving the prayer she was herself, just what she appeared to be, a lady. But as the trance condition came upon her and the guide took over the address a man's powerful voice rang out. Her whole character and personality changed.

The knowledge coming from the spirit world was proof in itself of the power of spirit. Meurig would ask for a subject to be suggested from the audience and then speak upon it for an hour or more. Then she would answer any questions put upon that subject for often another hour, being precise and knowledgeable. The quality of her mediumship was so high that such a helper could work through her without hindrance.

I have said it many times and will repeat it: unless the knowledge given in trance is greater than the medium can produce in the normal state, I see no need for trance. All the great trance mediums I have known have shown this change in personality and character. A greater knowledge than that of the medium has been demonstrated.

I learnt a great deal from Meurig, who always queried her mediumship. She was a kind and loving woman. It was she who started me looking into the mechanics of trance work. Her guide showed her clearly that he did not enter her body during trance but remained in the aura where the power is and they used just a small part of her brain; we were led to question further. This curiosity of hers led us to other questions and other answers.

It is like a chain reaction; the link to the physical body is through the etheric body, the secondary body. This is the body that St Paul spoke about as the spiritual body. There lies the power of mediumship — in the spiritual, not in the physical.

There have been so many friends who gave so much to the movement: work, time, money and above all loyalty. Some have given all they have. I remember them, not always by name because there have been so many, but "by their works they shall be known." That holds as good now as when it was first spoken!

In the past many young mediums were both gifted and working. I remember people like Tony Green, Lilian Nutter and George Bailey, all so young and dedicated, boy and girl mediums.

One was actually born blind. From the age of ten, he was

talking to Spirit and by twelve was travelling the country. What courage to travel around at such an early age, coping with a disability which would have limited so many people into their own home, their own little circle of friends.

Here was a young man so gifted that he was able to overcome this disability and seek to give the love and comfort of Spirit to those in need. They were strangers to him and yet he reached out and touched their lives.

He was able to make his links accurately without being able to see physically. I often wonder now just what he could see. Was it what the spirit world see? Mr Lowe, the blind medium of Wolverhampton, was able to see at one time and was able to describe what the recipient was wearing, but not ever knowing these things from earthly contact. What does the mind visualise then? Here was clairvoyance at its best. There are so many things we don't completely understand, but I feel we should be finding out.

Of course, there has always been a Spiritualism because Spiritualism is all about facts. It is about your being here, coming to the earth, living here, having a soul and about a God, which is not a man, but rather a power, a universal mind.

We shouldn't try to find a name for God, an identity, because we are limiting to earth terms a power which although of the earth is certainly not an earthly being.

There were always mediums who were very envious; there will always be a certain amount of jealousy. I brought in a certain style which was successful and popular. I was getting bookings where others were not so there was some tension, but not from the really good mediums.

Those who were successful in their own right and knew what they were doing didn't have time for or interest in being jealous. They didn't worry about anyone else because they knew their own job. There were quite a lot of professional mediums. They knew and got on with each other. They may not have liked each other, but that is a different thing.

Most worked on their own and in places like the Marylebone Spiritualist Association, now the Spiritualist Association of Great Britain. There were some who were popular. Of course, they got most of the work. It is better these days. Because of Stansted Hall, mediums have learned to work together more. There is more friendship between them, not the same competitive atmosphere as there was.

All mediums today — whether they are good or not — are in demand. They are better treated in some ways and welcomed to do readings in Spiritualist churches, which was not always the case. Longton church did not allow private sittings. I changed that, saying it must be allowed. This is the medium's bread and butter. It is right they should have this opportunity. We can afford to pay mediums more now, which is a good thing.

Although it is good that mediums are in demand, there is also a danger in this. Mediums had to prove themselves in the golden days. They would not get bookings if they were not good. These days it seems that too many people are accepted on the platforms long before they are ready.

I have known some marvellous characters. I remember Bertha Harris, an excellent medium, but she had a reputation for being a battle axe...and was! She and I just didn't get along at all. I was asked to take her service at a London crematorium.

Well, I went to take her service and took a lot of trouble because I was terrified in case she was going to appear. I sent up a thought, saying, "You can listen, but don't come." I got through the service. I said nice things, pressed the button so the coffin would go through, thinking to myself, "You're going now, Bertha." But she wouldn't go!

I pressed and pressed this button. Then suddenly Bertha appeared by my side. She stood there with her hands on her hips as if to say, "You dare!" Do you know, just for a minute, I didn't dare! She was a very powerful woman, was "Battling Bertha." The official, sitting at the back watching, got up so I gestured to him. He gestured back. "Well," I thought. "I will have another go." Before I could touch the button, Bertha shot through, all on her own — the coffin, that is.

It was as much as to say, "I am as strong now as I ever was." I swear Bertha had planned it all and was saying to herself, "I am better than you even now, Gordon Higginson!" Of course, there wasn't a thing I could do about it. She got the better of our last round!

Oh yes, we had some wonderful characters. We didn't all like each other, but had respect for each other's mediumship.

Grace Boyers was another excellent trance medium. I remember working with her in large halls where she held the audience spellbound with her wonderful oratory. They were the great days, the golden age, when it seemed that heaven had loaned to us great souls to come to this world to give such marvellous things.

These are times I will never forget. They have given to me such wonderful hope for the future of this world for I know that Spirit touches this world and have brought into it such souls.

Though Ena Twigg was a wonderful sensitive — she gave superb evidence — perhaps one of the greatest mediums whom I had the utmost admiration for was Estelle Roberts. Her mediumship was so brilliant that one felt very humble in her presence. I was privileged to have communication with her guide when she was in trance. I sat in her direct voice seance which was called the Red Cloud Circle, after her guide.

Then there was Helen Hughes, with whom I shared a platform in Glasgow. A brilliant trance medium as well as being clairaudient, Helen was such a dignified and delightful woman. When she spoke to you, it was like having clear water run through your mind.

Lilian Bailey was a friend of my mother. I often talked to her guide, Poppet, around our fireside in the most intimate and wonderful way. These people were the pillars — and still are. They have not left us, but continue working in the spirit world.

The names I have mentioned are only a few of the legion who prepared the ground for us today that we may be able to move forward and reach people in all parts of the world.

I saw the perfection to which they reached. I saw the dedication which ruled their lives. I was conscious of their tremendous humility, that they had a mission. It all changed my life because when you are young and in your twenties you look at other peoples' lives and begin to question your own.

I often wondered whether I had missed something in my own, but when I met these great personalities I realised they had something a little bit more than anybody else, although our lives can be very lonely and must be faced alone. Though we sometimes meet with abuse and the horrific things that people put before us, I would not change the path which was chosen for me. I would still go through it all again because I so believe that the power of Spirit is so needed in this world.

Chapter 19

SPIRIT DIRECTION

ALL my life I have been helped through direction and even intervention by the spirit world. I have often wondered about this and occasionally felt a little guilty when I hear about others, equally deserving, who have not enjoyed this privilege.

I came into exactly the right family to fulfil my destiny, but then I believe that everyone does no matter what that destiny may be, whether it is great in the eyes of the world or of apparently lesser importance.

I had spent time and effort and was helped by spirit inspiration in the rebuilding of my own church in Longton. We had a marvellously virile committee. Our members supported us throughout. During the late 1950s we had extensive alterations made in the structure.

We remained open through the alterations, which gave us a greater capacity and a large kitchen. We had worked hard after the war to re-establish a good and growing congregation. Our young were always strongly supportive, and we had two side windows dedicated specially for the children.

Professionally, I had been made a director of the chain of shoe stores where I had been a buyer for many years. This meant a dramatic reduction in the number of meetings I could take other than in my local area.

The number of requests being made for my services throughout the country made this an impossible situation so I sent up an appeal to the spirit world. I always had complete faith in my friends from this world and knew all would be well. I must wait and then act when the time was right.

Soon the opportunity was presented in the way of a small shop for sale in the Potteries. It was very run down, but I truly believed I would be able to make a success of running this.

My friend, Frank Tams, was willing to come into this venture with me and agreed to take on the greater part of the day-to-day work. This would mean I would have the time needed for my work as a medium. And so in 1957 I exchanged soles for souls.

Together we built up the business, sold it profitably and then did the same with another one. When I reached retirement age, I was able to give up business to devote all my time to Spiritualism.

I decided it was time to retire, but because of all the unpleasant experiences I had faced over the previous few years I realised I must have time and space to think about my future.

I went to Scotland by myself to find peace, strength and guidance. I found all three in that beautiful country. I have always loved Scotland and made many good friends there. There is a spiritual freedom in the quiet places and a spiritual strength in many of the people there which has been a great support to me many times in my career.

I think the point comes in every person's life when they must take time out, time to contemplate. Although I have always been so close to Spirit and have such joy in their constant companionship, I think even I sometimes lose sight of my mission.

There are times when life takes over. All the mundane things that happen to us and around us start to take on an importance they should not have. It is difficult to resist this when you have commitments to so many people, commitments made often so far in advance.

I am a person who likes stability. It sounds funny to say that when I live in the middle of change. I bought my house after the war and when I moved, only went just down the road. There I have happy memories of mother and my family. Although I have lost so many into Spirit, I feel they are still with me when I am alone.

I used to think a lot about my treasures, but have been burgled several times. Most of those things I valued were stolen. I was upset at the time because then I thought more about "things." Perhaps in growing older you lose sight of the material and look more to things of the Spirit.

Maybe it is just a self-defence. When objects of value, not monetary but of sentiment, are taken, some form of defence is needed. Things can be taken, destroyed or lost to sight, but that of the Spirit endures. To continue to be attached to that which is so very finite seems to be rather silly now.

If I was to be able to take something with me, I think I would perhaps choose a ring which was given to me by Vout Peters, a well-known medium. He always took it with him on platform. I used to do the same until I realised it was really too big and too showy.

If I believed in coffins, I would want it placed in there with me. It might be a little difficult, of course, because it was stolen. There were other belongings taken at that time and of far greater value, but that was the one I most regretted.

Anyway, I was led into the right job and from there into a business venture with Frank, who took most of the pressure from me. I was very lucky on both counts because although I have never become rich, I have not had to worry about my personal finances. Because I did not have this pressure from the material world, I was able to concentrate my energies where Spirit required.

I was born to be a medium and at first thought that was my destiny. Then I met Arthur Findlay, who lit a blaze of idealism for Stansted Hall within me, one which has never died.

It was really in the early part of 1970 I was to be helped — or led — into the dual nature of my life's work. I really wonder sometimes which way it was, but this is what happened.

I was taking the service at Portsmouth one Saturday evening and due at my own church on the Sunday afternoon. I decided to travel back through the night. I had done this a number of times, but it was a shock to find that I had, somehow, lost my directions. I was on my way to Stansted Hall!

I knew that Walter Sills and his wife May would be at the hall. Mr Sills was then union treasurer and, at that time, the acting manager of the hall. There would be no guests as it was closed during the winter months at that time until about April.

I rang to check they would be willing to give me a bed as I would be arriving rather late. I was fairly certain it would be all right because I knew Mr Sills quite well, and he was a very nice man, very kind. He waited up for me with tea and sandwiches. We spoke for a while about the union, of which I was then vice-president.

In the morning I got up and went downstairs. Mr Sills greeted me and to my surprise told me there was someone waiting to see me. The person had told him I would know he was coming.

Well I didn't. Indeed, I should not have been there that day and did not know until late the previous night that I would be. I really had no idea who it could be and said so. Mr Sills had asked the visitor to wait in the library so I had breakfast before going in to find out who it was and what he wanted.

Quietly, I looked round the door. To my surprise, my visitor was a monk in a brown habit and sandals. I was quite astonished. Well, I didn't know any monks! I went back to Mr Sills and said: "I don't know of any monk who would want to see me. I didn't expect any visitors. No one knows I am here."

"Well," Mr Sills replied, "he asked for you by name."

I was really curious by now. I went back in and asked the monk what he wanted. "Did you know that you were to meet me here?" he asked. I said "No." Then the monk inquired, "Where should you have been this morning?" I told him I ought to have been at home, and explained what had happened, that I had lost my way.

"Didn't you stop to think that perhaps there was some reason why you should have to stay here the night?" asked my visitor. "I have come to bring you a message." "Oh dear," thought I. "This is a peculiar thing to be happening." But I was very curious.

The monk went on: "You have a mission in life. You have turned down an opportunity that is important to the mission you have in life."

"Well," I said, "the only thing I can think of that I have refused to do is to stand as the president of the SNU." I couldn't think of anything else. I very seldom found it in me to say "No." to people. It always seems such a hard and final word to me.

"We would like you to reconsider," said the monk. "You have a job to do, a mission to fulfil. A lot will depend on what you intend to do." I asked if he would mind if I spoke with the treasurer of the union as I could not give him my answer straight away.

I went out and said to Mr Sills: "This man is crazy. I can't possibly take on the presidency. I have a very demanding job; I have my own church; I am the vice-president; I work for the college; I take services. I can't possibly take on any more."

I cannot remember wondering what it had to do with a strange monk whether I should or should not accept the presidency as it all happened quite quickly and there was an air of unreality about the whole thing.

Bill Sills offered to speak to the monk for me. We both returned to the library — to find he had disappeared! We looked around, but there was no sign of him. We searched the hall, the grounds, even down to the village asking if people had seen anyone dressed like a monk. They must have wondered if we were crazy, but no one had seen him.

I rather wanted Mr Sills to hear what the monk had to say because I could hardly believe it myself. I also wanted him to be a witness. This particular experience, which had been shared in part by Mr Sills, left me shaken. You see, there was no way the monk could have left the library without our seeing him. We were standing on the stairs, opposite the only door.

We had searched because it seemed he must have slipped out. We knew in our hearts he could not have done, but still wanted to accept the normal rather than the supernormal. That, of course, is human nature.

I decided to write to Richard Ellidge, the then general secretary, and tell him I withdrew my objection and would now stand for office. Again, I believed it would only be for a few years. How strange it is that 22 years later I should still be holding the same office! And what changes there are.

At that time, we were practically bankrupt. The hall owed thousands of pounds with no clear view that we could ever pay our debts. There was no obvious way out of our dilemma. I did not want to be the president who was responsible for winding up the SNU yet here I was accepting this position.

Now, we still have financial problems. Often we work from week to week with few reserves, but we have paid our debts. The college has become a symbol of Spiritualism that is accepted all over the world. From having a few guests per week and a limited season we now fill the hall most weeks of the year.

Foreign students come in chartered plane-loads. Name any country and we have people who travel from there to take what we can give at Stansted, something they cannot get anywhere else in the world. I believe that Stansted Hall is the centre of Modern Spiritualism in the world.

I also believe that the SNU was chosen to take on this responsibility because it teaches pure Spiritualism. It has no prefixes, but a definite message that all religions can accept. There is nothing they cannot accept because life after death can be proven.

It is a fact. Therefore, we have that uniting principle to bring people together. I believe there is a greater force than man operating in this world. This force — which always has been and always will be — has moved men and women in their hearts and minds to bring good into this world.

I think of all the great people throughout history who have been able to prove to us they have these great powers, superhuman powers, because they are involved spiritually and have a spiritual destiny. When I think of these, I feel humble at the part I have played. When I consider how much help I have been given, I also wonder just how much help they were given and whether they realised.

I always, in times of trouble or confusion, went to my mother. She was a great medium. I would go to her and say: "May I talk to those in the spirit world who are your guides and comforters? I would like to put some questions to them." They did not fail me.

I was also privileged on many occasions to do likewise to the guide of Maurice Barbanell, Silver Birch. He was always so kind, so helpful. At this time, when I was simply not sure if I was going the right way, I needed his assurance.

It seemed it was always when I needed advice most that the invitation to attend the Silver Birch circle came. I have always been given so much help from the spirit world. I could not have fulfilled my responsibilities to the movement without the help received over the years.

It was Silver Birch who taught me a great deal about life. It was this great guide who comforted and encouraged me at a time when I was very low and I wondered if I had had enough, if I could actually bear to carry on.

Sometimes, I did not seem to be strong enough to bear all the enmity around me. People can be very unkind, very hurtful and destructive. If it had not been for my own guides and those others with whom I had a contact, I do not know how I could have coped.

It was a time of great trauma for all of us. We were criticised for spending £80.000 without first having a feasibility study carried out by experts. Bertha Harris stated in "Psychic News" that she tried to dissuade Arthur Findlay in the way that he determined. This was to make the college a place of psychic and spiritual studies.

Bertha stated she had received messages from our pioneers urging that the college be sold and the proceeds used to buy another one in a more accessible area which could be maintained more economically. She claimed that Arthur had communicated, saying he was disturbed about the financial situation.

Bertha and I did not get on very well, but I doubted if she would tell an absolute lie so I worried. I always said that I was right, and believed I was, especially when Spirit were relaying the message.

Had I made a terrible error? Of course, Arthur would be concerned about the financial situation. So was I and many others, but I could not believe he would give in so easily. I did not believe he would suggest selling the hall. Not in a million years would I believe this.

All my life I owed no one a penny. Now my name was connected with this appalling debt. Something would have to be done as the SNU, which I respected, was being drained financially. I felt personally responsible to find the way out of these problems.

I believe Silver Birch is probably the most highly evolved guide to reach this earth plane in modern centuries. His medium was the highly respected and well-known editor of "Psychic News." He was, though, far more than that.

Barbie, as he was known to friends, was also called "Mr Spiritualism." He had a wonderful relationship with Silver Birch. Often they disagreed on certain matters. Thus, when Silver Birch was "in control," one opinion would be expressed and then Barbie would be the opposite when all was equal and Silver Birch had withdrawn. It is the most wonderful example of how two personalities can work in co-operation together.

At the Hannen Swaffer Home Circle — named after the famous journalist and Spiritualist — the words of Silver Birch gave me hope and comfort. Here is just a small part of what he told me:

"I know, perhaps, better than others, the hard roads that mediums have to travel. The sacrifices which have to be made; the exterior presented to the public hiding the crucifixion that so often happens.

"You know, those who have work to do must expect hardships to be part of the trials and tests to ensure that the mettle is strong enough for the tasks you have to perform. You are helping far more than you realise."

I asked Silver Birch whether we were going in the right direction. He replied: "Sometimes, I think our biggest troubles are not those who are without, but it is within. The ones who have a little knowledge can be the stumbling blocks. Alas, vanity and pride play their baleful parts. Would that the pristine vision which attracted them in the first place did not become so faded and gloomy as time goes on. There is work for all to do.

"So, do your best. When you fall down, pick yourself up. That is the reason for your falling down, so that you can get on your feet again. When you are convinced that what you are doing is right, do it. Let those who disagree with you go their own way..." Silver Birch went on to say that there would have to be changes made, adding: "You will come through. Your organisation will survive."

I really needed to be told this at that time. It helped to cement my resolve to do this work and to win through. I knew it could be done, and I had an idea of how to start. My problem was this: would others feel the same way? Could we dispel the apathy and generate a massive interest and support for Spiritualism and the union?

Chapter 20

POLL PROVES IT

ALTHOUGH I have made a success of my material life, I have always considered that the spiritual work was my priority. This is hardly surprising considering that from the time I an able to remember I have been in close touch with the spirit world. Often in my youth, I was unable to distinguish between those who were in this life and those who had already passed.

It was when I started meeting and working with some of the great mediums of this century that, looking at their great dedication, I started to question my own worth and my own life. It seemed to me that heaven had loaned to us such great mediums, such spiritual beings, for a purpose. It gave me such a hope for humanity to know they had touched this earth.

I was a fortunate person in that I was born to a purpose in life, but I realised through my contact with these mediums that such a purpose brings with it great responsibility.

I had been used to talking with my mother's guides as well as my own, but I was also privileged to sit around the fire talking with Poppet, the child guide of Lilian Bailey. She was a good friend of my mother for they had trained together at Longton. To some it may seem extraordinary that we had such an intimate contact with those from the spirit world, but that was the atmosphere in which I was raised. I will always be grateful for those experiences.

A lot of people have wondered why I have links with the Greater World Christian Spiritualist Association. Some have even "wondered" to my face! Well, I believe that Spirit comes first and organisations are man-made. And I tell them this. Then they go away quite happy because I am right, you know!

I knew Winifred Moyes, the association's founder, as a teenager and, later, upon two occasions, was asked to work with her and her guide Zodiac. My mother always had contact with Christianity for this was my father's religion. Although he gave up his active participation so that my mother could travel to the different churches to work on Sundays, he and she agreed when they married that all their children would have knowledge of both religions, Spiritualism and Christianity.

Miss Moyes was an excellent trance medium so I felt privileged to be on the platform with her. My mother was one of the first mediums to get a diploma from the Greater World. One year, after I had worked for them, they sent me one as well! I thought how kind it was of them, and admit I thought no more of it. But it was kind because I was quite young then.

I have been a guest speaker at many of their meetings in the past. They have always treated me kindly, even when we disagreed with each other. I remember once, as a teenager, that I did a double demonstration with my mother in my home town. Miss Moyes had been the speaker and was first class.

I first spoke at one of the Greater World dinners in 1980. I had just finished working at Caxton Hall and was a little later than I had intended. As I arrived, the porter asked me, "Exit or Survival?" I thought he was being facetious, but he was not. There was another meeting that night for those interested in voluntary euthanasia — and the organisation is called Exit.

Looking back further, when I was just 16 years old I was asked to work at the Picton Hall, in Liverpool. Hannen Swaffer was the speaker, one of our most brilliant. He had a wonderful mind, so quick, so sharp. The hall was packed to capacity. Many were turned away.

Swaff, as I later knew him, was given a standing ovation. I think that this night is one of the great memories of my life. I worked really well. At the end, I came off the platform and stood there waiting for congratulations. I watched as every person crowded round just wanting to be near or to speak to Swaff.

I got to speak to him in the end. He said to me — and I have never forgotten this — "I have given a lifetime to the study of mediumship and Spiritualism. One day you will make a very good medium. Perhaps one of the best, but just always remember this: all the knowledge and experience I have will only cover the head of a pin!"

If ever I start to feeling that I know it all, I remember the words of that great man to a young medium. Swaff was not condescending. He knew the dangers which are faced by mediums; he knew how little we ever get to know, even when we think we have it all, that when we have learnt all we think there is to learn, there is still a lifetime of learning in front of us.

This, I feel, was the golden age of mediumship as there were so many who were so very good. I worked with Ena Twigg on many occasions. After the war, we demonstrated together to 8,000 people in four weeks.

Four meetings were arranged in Manchester, Birmingham, Glasgow and Newcastle-on-Tyne. This was a joint venture between "Psychic News" and "Reynolds News."

At each of these there was a panel, volunteers from the audience, who questioned recipients of messages concerning their accuracy and to make certain there could have been no collusion. Then the members of the audience were asked to fill in ballot papers to show whether they were convinced that there was life after death.

The overwhelming verdict was "Yes!" Well, we had been very good and the evidence was quite outstanding. I remember that at one meeting Ena was giving a message from a John Andrews who had been in the Merchant Navy and lost in the Atlantic on a convoy route. The information was denied by the recipient. Only one small part of the message, which contained some remarkable details, would he accept.

Fortunately, this did not detract from the impact of the demonstration, although it left Ena a little puzzled. The true recipient of the message was seated just a few seats along the row. He, a Mr Ball, contacted "Reynolds News" the next day to confirm that he could accept all the details exactly as given.

This is one of the dangers of large meetings and is very disconcerting when it happens. Of course, ideally, it offers wonderful proof that Spirit are communicating as individuals and not as a result of the link with the recipient. However, it can be worrying for the medium who is sure that the link is accurate, but getting a denial.

At least 20 per cent of the people who filled in a questionnaire stated that they had never attended a Spiritualist meeting before. This was marvellous because it meant we were attracting new people. They might not go on to attend the local church. But at least they had some experience of Spiritualism to look back upon.

In Birmingham we had an interruption by a young man who had been picketing outside the hall. It was while Harold Vigurs was answering questions from the audience. "You are working with the devil!" he shouted. The audience laughed; they were at the meeting and knew otherwise.

The young man persisted and actually carried out an "exorcism," commanding the spirits to come out of us, the mediums, in the name of Jesus Christ! I was young then and felt he deserved the laughter which greeted this action.

Perhaps he did, but I do feel so very sorry for these people who live in such a devil-infested world. They do not appreciate the unlimited wonders that God has bestowed upon us.

It was at a large meeting for the Freedom Fund that I first worked with Harold Vigurs. He remained a good friend to me through many years until his passing. It was through his introduction to the London area that I was asked to take the May Convention Meeting — and was asked back about four years in succession. I was the only medium to be asked like this. It was a great honour.

In 1949, we took the Armistice Day celebrations together. This was a huge meeting at Deansgate, Manchester. Harold spoke about the way in which Spirit communicated to bring comfort. He told the story about how he was sitting with two friends when there was a knock at the door and a woman stood there. She had come for comfort, having recently lost her husband.

Harold subdued his first reaction, which was to tell the lady to return later as he was busy, and invited her in. Suddenly, one of his companions started to describe a man whom the lady admitted sounded like her husband. "He is trying to impart wisdom," said his friend. The woman was confused, asking, "Why? What makes you think that?" "Because he is holding in his hand an eye, and the eye denotes wisdom," said he.

The woman broke down in tears. When she recovered, she explained she now knew this was indeed her husband. He had had a glass eye. When she heard this, together with the description which had been given, she knew it could be no other.

Mediums must give what they are getting. They do not always realise its importance. It is Spirit who do the work. Harold could illustrate the simple truths of our work in just such a way. He was a most loving man. I enjoyed the times when I worked with him for I knew that the philosophy of spiritual truth would truly be expounded.

That night I was able, through the spirit world, to help a man in the audience who was so very frightened of the future. I knew I was linked with Old Hall Lane and the name Priscilla. I found the recipient, a gentleman by the name of Smith. I confirmed that he was the right person by giving other details which he was able to accept. Then Spirit asked me to tell him: "No matter what you are told, you must rest assured that you will recover. You must take care, but what happened recently, a sort of collapse, will not happen again."

Later, the gentleman explained and said that it was "the most evidential message I have ever received. And it is the best news I have had in a long time." He would be able to face his life with new courage, knowing he was not in danger of another collapse and would be able to take care of his family. How wonderful to know that this man would go forward and take up the threads of his life without the fear that had haunted him.

There were so many big meetings in those days. People were turned away from the doors because they didn't arrive in time to get a seat. It was not just the demonstration, but the quality of the speakers which attracted them. I always used to take the Remembrance Service at the Victoria Halls in Hanley.

Hazel, my sister, always came with me. Mother wouldn't train her as a medium because she said Hazel did not have the right temperament for it, but she used to come with me when I worked.

She and I sat together for a while with an old friend of our family, Gertie Sherratt. She was there when my friend Choo Chow first used me as his instrument. He was almost as strong that first time as he was later on. Sometimes, I feel so grateful for the helpers

I have. I couldn't have done these meetings at such a young age without their being so strong.

Hazel was also present when I worked on the same platform with Godfrey Wynn and Lord Dowding. I was still young and felt proud she was there to see me working with such great people. I worked several times with Lord Dowding, a marvellous speaker. He looked very ordinary, but he could speak! I think the last time I heard him was at Stratford Town Hall in 1959 where we worked together.

In 1953, it was decided that the centenary of English Spiritualism should be celebrated. There was to be a full week's meetings in Keighley because that is really where British Spiritualism started.

Most people think of Mrs Haydn who worked in the South and got most of the publicity when they recall the first workers. It was, in fact, a Darlington man, David Richmond, who trained in America who got our movement going in the way that we think of it today. He and Mr Weatherhead started a group in Keighley and so lit a torch which has never dimmed. From time to time we face our problems, but the torch burns!

I was very pleased and proud to be asked to take the first service, a Saturday demonstration. It went very well. The hall was absolutely crowded. The organisers crammed in as many as possible because people had travelled from all over to be there.

The next day, there was a Lyceum session in the afternoon. The Lyceum was always strong in the Midlands so it was a very good turn out. In the evening, Harry Edwards gave a healing service. Harry did so much in those years to help the union whenever he could.

Medium Ivy Northage and Charles Quastel were just two of the workers during the week. Of course, Percy Wilson was there, not only because he was the president of the SNU, but because he had personal links with Keighley through his grandfather. I think that there are more people in the Midlands and North who can trace their family history back in Spiritualism than in the Southern regions.

People turned out in numbers for these meetings. They did not just come for the clairvoyance, but to show their support for their chosen way of life. It was wonderful to see them and to work in that atmosphere. It seemed as if the spirit world had turned out in force to wish us well.

At one of the first meetings that Mr Quastel took after becoming union president we attracted over 1,000 people. Just think: over 1,000 — and the attraction was not just the clairvoyance but the speaker. Charles spoke of the need of Spiritualism to spearhead religious thought throughout the world, to fight against the growing apathy. It was a speech to remember. Imagine the power that had built by the time I stood up.

Going further north, I always loved working in Glasgow, and often gave trance and physical demonstrations there. At one meeting, the first message was accepted by two different ladies. I could not separate them. I kept giving a little more and a little more — and they kept saying "Yes" to everything.

I was almost in despair; the people loved it and were laughing as I tried again and again. In the end we realised the situation. The two ladies were sisters. They had come separately, were sitting at opposite sides of the hall and therefore could not see each other. Once we realised their relationship, it all made sense.

It is very difficult sometimes, when you are looking back to separate events, to recall what happened one year and what happened another. All the meetings were exciting in their own way. But I think if I had to pick out any that were really different it would be those at the Albert Hall. First it was so big! The rows and tiers of people just seemed to go on and on. It was lucky that I had been so well trained and been given so much opportunity to work in large venues.

I did the first, I think, in 1970 or 1971. I was booked to take all the others until we no longer booked the Albert Hall. We did go on to other halls, but it was never the same. Now we no longer hold a large meeting on Remembrance Day to recall those who passed. Perhaps it is as well for we in Spiritualism never put them aside, do we?

Though I was the president of the largest Spiritualist organisation in Britain, when I was invited to take part in the Memorial Service at the Royal Albert Hall I was so pleased. I had been used to taking large meetings for so many years, but this seemed to be an accolade. I know that Mother was pleased.

She would never travel far. Travelling did not agree with her nor she with it — and she made no exception for this event. I think she might have done, but she was no longer a young woman. Hazel was there and so were many of my friends. I really needed their support.

I always do get nervous before meetings. When I was quite young, the papers accused me of being theatrical, but it was more nervous tension than deliberate gestures. I never have got over that feeling before going on. At my age, I don't think I will, not now!

The last meeting but one at the Albert Hall was in 1974 and really quite superb. Hunter Mackintosh, then president of the Spiritualist Association of Great Britain, chaired the meeting. He was very relaxed, which helped us tremendously. Hunter spoke about the fallacy of death and about the fact that our service was not a remembrance so much as a reunion.

Psychic artist Coral Polge and I were to use the Master Screen at this meeting. It was massive. Maurice Barbanell called it one of the great views of Spiritualism. Doris Collins was actually booked to work with Coral, but we changed around and Doris worked on her own. It turned out absolutely right to be done that way for the meeting was a tremendous success.

Coral and I had first used a big screen like this some six months previously in Derby when we were filmed by a Japanese camera crew. That was such a success, in spite of these little men scurrying all over the place. At one point they actually went behind Coral's equipment to film her face as she was working.

Tom Johanson said at the time how well the demonstration had worked, and that he wished he had arranged the Albert Hall team rather differently. Coral was supposed to work with Doris Collins whilst I was to work alone. Tom had not realised how well Coral and I could work together.

I arrived at the Albert Hall in very good time. I was always so nervous, but think that this time I was even more so. I went in to find out where I was to work and where I was to dress. Tom and Coral were there. Tom, as general secretary of the Spiritualist Association of Great Britain, was very involved in the organisation of the evening.

One of the first problems was that Doris was not sure about working in tandem with Coral. Tom suggested that we change around. I was quite happy about this, feeling quite confident that Coral and I would be good together.

The Rev David Kennedy, who had written a book detailing survival evidence from his dead wife, couldn't be with us, but my old friend Harry Edwards made a marvellous job of deputising for him. He was a beautiful speaker. Everyone thinks of him these days as a healer, but he was very good on the platform. Actually, Harry was a minister of the SNU. Although we had our differences over the years it did not spoil our feelings for each other.

Harry spoke so movingly about a 12-year-old Birmingham girl who had benefited from healing. She was taken to her local rector with advanced cancer of the upper leg after her doctor said her only chance was spiritual healing. The vicar took her to Shere. The latest news was that she was slowly improving.

Additionally, Harry reminded everyone of the tragedies of world starvation and yet how we in this country have so much. He linked this with spiritual hunger, which must be filled.

Hunter Mackintosh then introduced Doris Collins, who had worked at the previous year's service. She was very good. I think Spirit must have done a little work to arrange things so it was I who worked with Coral and not Doris. I think really that she was better on her own.

There was quite a stir when people realised that the screen behind us was to show Coral's spirit-inspired drawings. It was the first time it had been used for such a purpose, and meant that everyone could see clearly.

I cannot recall all the links I had, but some were highlighted in "Psychic News." I remembered them when I looked back.

One sketch was of a young girl. I linked it with the name of Roberts, Brentwood Terrace and Bertha still on the earth. With these details, the recipient was able to recognise that he was the one for whom the message was intended. The sketch was actually of a neighbour's daughter so he took it home to give to them. The man would know which neighbour because I was able to give the correct name and where their house was situated.

One name given was Grimstone, but it should have been

Grimbaldstone. Details of the street and inhabitants were given plus Paul, the name of the boy in the drawing. The recipient said Paul was still living, although the details were correct.

Someone who knew the name Kendall was asked to identify the next drawing. He was given many details of his family and identified the drawing as being very like his grandmother. This recipient had never attended a service before and was sceptical. He identified the phone number given as indeed being connected with a school — and as one he had used just that day!

Then I heard Spirit say "Muriel" and "Sutton Road." I was shown a car and could see the number, which I gave. A man accepted the details which I had given so far, but the number did not belong to the car. It was the number of his house, which I had also described. I naturally thought it belonged to the car because I saw it on the vehicle. Spirit showed me all around where he lived, his roses, his caravan, and it was all accepted as correct. I have worked with Coral many times. She is an excellent medium.

The following year Coral and I again worked very successfully as a team whilst Billy Redmond was the speaker. The reporter from "Psychic News" thought that Hunter Mackintosh's address was perhaps the better of the two. He was probably right, but Billy had a tremendous compassion and that came over very well. Of course, he was such a wonderful clairvoyant.

Alas, that was the last time Spiritualists met at the Albert Hall. It was getting so very expensive to hire, and the organisation was a tremendous task. The Spiritualist Association did a marvellous job — and the publicity was good for our movement.

Over the years some of our top mediums and speakers worked at the Albert Hall. The experience was overwhelming really, but the atmosphere generated by all those people lifted the vibrations so that the demonstrations were always first class.

We even got paid. It was a token payment of only about £10, but that wasn't bad for the 1970s. Really, the honour and experience were enough. We worked for Spiritualism...and it created such a good impression that we were able to hire the Albert Hall for our own form of remembrance.

Although that last meeting was memorable, I must recall the meeting we had at the Albert Hall in 1973. Harry Edwards had celebrated his 80th birthday only two days previously. All the speakers paid tribute to the extent of his work.

Barbie, who chaired the meeting, named Harry as "The most famous healer in the world." I can't think of anyone there who would argue the point. Dennis Fayre, then chairman of the National Federation of Spiritual Healers, presented Harry with a bust in his likeness, but the most popular presentation was from Bulawayo Spiritualist Church in Rhodesia where Harry had recently visited. Ken Oakes had made a cast of his hands.

How the audience loved it as Barbie paraphrased the television programme announcing, "These are your hands Harry!" It was a meeting which sparkled with friendship, laughter and true spiritual interchange.

I worked quite a lot with Harry, one of those who offered their services so willingly and freely when we were trying to raise money to keep the union afloat.

One day we held an afternoon and evening service in Plymouth. Over 800 people attended. Many came for the wonderful help Harry was able to give. He was a marvellous man, one who worked so very hard for the movement, although healing was his first love.

I believe he would have made an excellent physical medium. That day, one patient was a lady virtually unable to walk onto the stage. But after Harry's healing, she practically skipped off, smiling in sheer joy. The pain which she had suffered for so long had gone. Her spine had been like a board. Now she could bend it normally.

Olive Burton assisted him; she was very good with ears. One woman had been deaf in one ear for 25 years and had minimal hearing in the other. Doctors agreed they could do nothing. Within minutes she could hear the faint click of Harry's fingers.

There were so many. There always are! I think healing is so very important in our movement. The body and the spirit must be in harmony for when one is out of line, the other cannot grow to full strength.

I was in good form as well! This was only one of the many meetings that were arranged between "Psychic News" and the union. Such a lot of effort had gone into these. I know that Spirit were co-operating to make these a success.

Barbie arranged that back copies of "Psychic News" and leaflets about Spiritualism would be delivered to every local household in the area where we were working.

This was yet another occasion when I could not separate two people claiming the same message only to find that they were related. Usually I am directed to an area in which to work rather than direct to the recipient.

I had started to work like this years ago when I first realised that I was being groomed for larger meetings as this is the only reasonable way to work when there is such a crowd you cannot see who you are talking to. I suffered quite a lot of criticism due to this and because the details I sometimes gave were recorded at one point or another and could, possibly, have been read and remembered.

At this meeting, Spirit were obviously going to prove to those critics they could give that sort of detail and identify personally where the details belonged. I think I was wrong only twice in identifying the recipient of the messages.

I must mention that "Psychic News" and I may have had our differences, but that never interfered with the support that was given to me as the president and the union as an organisation. I often thought they were wrong and said so; they reciprocated when they thought I was wrong. That quite often made me cross, but we remained friends after all.

In 1981, it was my sad duty and pleasure to honour my old friend Barbie at the Friends Meeting House in London. He passed quite suddenly, a shock to us all. We know that our days here are numbered but he had been part of Spiritualism for 60 years and would be sorely missed.

David Dutton, then Chairman of the Spiritual Truth Foundation, chaired the meeting. Over a thousand people attended. Sylvia Barbanell was there, looking absolutely lovely. She was always such a support to Barbie. We gave him a grand farewell. Several others besides myself were aware that he was there himself to enjoy the occasion.

My friend M.H.Tester, who was also a director of Psychic Press, gave the tribute. I don't think anyone could have done it better. It was a moving and emotional tribute. He spoke of Barbie standing up on a soap box at Hyde Park's Speakers' Corner. Mr Tester recalled that Barbie was the longest serving minister in the union and how much he had done to promote Spiritualism within the law and the press.

For a long time it was a closely kept secret that Barbie was the medium through whom Silver Birch was able to communicate. It was in the home circle of Hannen Swaffer that these two unlikely partners worked in harmony for so many years, one so very human and, he would be the first to admit, a little cynical, rough at times; the other so full of love and wisdom.

It just shows, as like attracts like, that we cannot always judge people for what they seem to be. To work so well and for so long with one of the wisest guides we have known this century there must have been so much love and compassion in my friend Barbie which wasn't always obvious.

He was a crusader of note, an author, editor, catalyst and a very human being. Barbie could be really mean with money and yet extraordinarily generous. I was pleased and very proud that I was part of this service of recognition.

Joe Benjamin worked first. He had a very direct way of working and was able to give evidence in a code which had been arranged with the recipient of the message before the passing of the communicator.

It was a loving service, one during which the spirit world brought forward humour. Giving clairvoyance, I spoke to one woman whose mother in Spirit gave away the fact that her daughter was the one who used to teach the parrot to swear. She was laughing and blushing as she admitted that what her mother said was true, but that no-one had known she was the culprit. Everyone wondered how on earth the parrot was learning such things!

Barbie would have loved such a message since he had a sense of humour and would not have wanted to be remembered without some laughter.

In 1990, we decided we would have meetings up and down the country to celebrate the centenary year of our national organisation. The Spiritualists' National Union started out as the National Federation, but had changed the name in 1901. Nevertheless, it was 100 years since our pioneers had succeeded in forming into a union — and I was determined that this should not pass unnoticed.

All the district councils had been asked to start making their own arrangements: these would be co-ordinated through the Publicity Committee. I soon realised it was necessary to upgrade this committee to a Standing Committee status.

This meant the chairman would be a director of the union, part of the National Executive Committee and therefore have greater powers of authority and discretion. I decided to ask medium and minister Jean Bassett to take on this task because I felt she was the right person for this job.

The year's celebrations started with a grand meeting at Wembley. Jean booked March 31 as this is, of course, Hydesville Day. I have always thought that we should make far more of Hydesville Day in Spiritualism. After all, that was when we accept Modern Spiritualism really started.

I really think it is time we celebrated our own anniversaries instead of those of other religions. I know that most religions do centre their events around the natural seasons of the earth, but we should have at least one which we regard as special.

The hall at Wembley holds 2,500 people — and we nearly filled it. We did not confine the people we booked to work just to those from the union. This day was, I felt, one to be shared with all Spiritualists in strength and unity. We started at noon and went right through until 10 o'clock at night.

There were flags and banners, singing and healing. People came from all over the country. Some actually travelled from abroad just to share the day with us. After I opened the day, Professor Archie Roy gave a wonderfully humorous talk. Coral Polge and Stephen O'Brien demonstrated their gifts of psychic art and clairvoyance respectively.

Then Ray and Joan Branch showed how they did healing from the platform. Our churches and the Guild of Spiritualist Healers also had healers on the platform, but a special room had been set aside throughout the day where they did the bulk of their work. It just shows how needed this is as there was no time during the day when there were not people waiting to be seen.

In the evening I had arranged that all the districts, branches and members of the National Executive Committee would be represented on the platform. My good friend Eric Hatton provided a fanfare to welcome me. I think that people quite liked that little touch. We didn't want to be too solemn because meetings like this should be joyful occasions.

Sir George Trevelyan gave the most wonderful spiritual address whilst another good medium friend of many years, Mary Duffy, worked with me. The atmosphere was electric...and the evidence just flowed. This does illustrate the point I have tried to make through this book: when you are with Spirit, there is no need to worry.

The raising of the consciousness to meet your own spirit energy which then blends with the energy of the spirit world really happens. It is as if the world itself changes and you are no longer conscious of time or space. I think that large meetings can be successful in this day, but you need workers who are trained to be ready for those occasions — and it must be done with spiritual, not material, intent.

Chapter 21

I AM ACCUSED

I KNOW that many of our top mediums have been accused of fraud. I vaguely sympathised with them until it happened to me. Then I knew the nightmare they went through.

The work I had done over the years proved beyond a shadow of doubt that my link with the spirit world is a very special and detailed one. To say, to shout, silently to scream "I don't need to cheat!" proved nothing.

I suppose that when you have held the position of top mediumship for so many years, there will always be somebody, somewhere who will want to pull you down. That somebody could never have been on the receiving end or they would not in a hundred years put another person through the trauma I and other mediums have endured.

My whole being hurt. My pride in being a good medium felt besmirched. Nevertheless, these things happened in my life. I cannot ignore and fail to record this.

I have, however, also recorded the only retaliation I was able to make — a special "trial" demonstration set up to test my abilities.

Of course, I insisted that the union had to follow through on these complaints. It was important for everyone to realise that even though I was one of the best known mediums in the country and worked for the SNU that all mediums are responsible and subject to the same rules.

People had always been astounded at the way I was able to give the names, addresses and other details from the spirit world, but it came from my early training with my mother. She insisted upon a degree of excellence. I worked very hard to develop my abilities.

One December, I agreed to work under test conditions. Charles Quastel arranged that I would not know where I was going until I actually reached my destination.

Mr T. Hemwood collected me from my home in Longton. We travelled by train to Derbyshire. The tickets had been purchased without my knowledge so I had no prior information. The committee of the church was not told who the medium was to be until three days prior to the meeting.

With two others, Mr Quastel met us at Derby station to ensure that I had no contact with any person or access to any information before going to the church, which turned out to be at Belper in Derbyshire.

The meeting started at 7 pm and was recorded verbatim. I still have the records. Afterwards the messages were carefully analysed by members of the union. They took eight long months to make their official statement.

When Mr Ellidge, the general secretary of the SNU, gave the results it was recognised that the demonstration was a first class experiment and he appealed to all the top mediums to be likewise tested.

So many ordinary Spiritualists wrote in my defence. Of course, my mother sprang to my defence. She had always defended me in this life: she knew my integrity .Harold Vigurs quoted instances of evidence given that could not have been either known or obtained through psychic links or ESP. This latter theory had been suggested as a solution by Evan Powell.

"We cannot," he said, "put a limit on how far Gordon's psychic faculty works, but his reputation cannot be sullied by such isolated incidents." It was such an unhappy time for me. Any medium who has been falsely accused will know the mental trauma which this causes.

Any medium in the public eye can be singled out for accusations of fraud, particularly, as in my case, when the information they are supplying is so very detailed. If you get any of the details wrong, there are some people who will think you cheated. But if you get everything right, they will also think you have cheated.

I have always tried to ignore these accusations or at least not to respond to them in public. Even now I think this was the best policy, although, naturally, there have been times when I have betrayed some of the hurt that I feel when this sort of thing happens.

I had to go through a similar situation in the middle of the 1970s. That was even worse as I was union president. The work load I had was staggering. The papers had a field day. I announced I would withdraw from public work, except in my own area. Perhaps I should not have reacted, but I did. I was hurt. All I could think of was to retire. The union members were very good. Yes, we do have some wonderful people in our movement.

I was accused that during a service at Bristol I gave messages to people whose names were in the church records. I would have had to have known where to find the records and moved several rows of chairs to get at them. While doing this I would be in view of anyone coming into the church or find keys to unlock the kitchen where there was a raffle list!

The accusations made had come from inside our movement — and this did hurt. They were made on conjecture and that hurt even more. They were sent to national newspapers: that hurt not just me but Spiritualism. It is no wonder really that I wanted to give up, to move out from centre stage and live out my life in peace.

I was not informed of the complaint before, but left to find out from Sunday papers in the middle of conference. I couldn't attend that day's session. I know I would have found support, but think that kindness at that point would have destroyed me completely. It was as much as I could do to keep going.

Again I asked that we should follow through on this complaint. Because I was president, everything had to be done to the letter and took some time to be completed. When the tribunal which cleared me of all charges met, it did not consist of union people. I wanted impartial individuals who could not be said were prejudiced in my favour. There were three, two barristers and Harry Smith from the Greater World Association.

Coral Polge was a great help to me at that time when all I wanted to do was give up. She and I were booked to take a large meeting at Gravesend, which was to be chaired by George Cranley, just after all this adverse publicity. I was persuaded that I must not let them down for all the tickets had been sold in advance. Everyone turned up; there was not a seat empty. Many were turned away.

One of our contacts was for the treasurer of the local Spiritualist church. Coral drew his uncle. I correctly named the recipient, his cottage and gave further details. As at Bristol, this information must have been in the church records. Again, as at Bristol the recipient was not in the hall.

This time, though, there was an important difference; I did not instigate the contact. Coral drew the treasurer's uncle, even included his bowler hat and mentioned his old dog. I merely linked and found the contact through my link with Spirit, and given, as always, the information about the communicator. I even mentioned how he used to throw his hat onto the gate post as he came home. How else could such information be given other than from Spirit?

What many did not know was how tight my schedule was. Often, I arrived an hour before a meeting. There was no way I would have had time to check or gather this information other than by means of spirit communication.

Yes, there were times when I wanted to be alone. I was often tired and needed that time of quiet before going onto the platform. People do not always realise that they are demanding. They are careful not to ask for messages or anything like that, but don't realise that sometimes being pleasant is demanding when a person is tired or tense to start with.

The names were not always given easily. I remember one incident in Hanley church where a man — he had never been in a Spiritualist church before — took some time before he would admit that Albert and Louisa were his parents, and that they had kept the Honey Wall some years before their passing.

He did in the end, but it was hard work. Spirit were right. I was right. And he did admit it in the end.

Magician Charles Cardell challenged me to name an article sealed into a silver box. He offered £1,000, but I have never accepted these sort of challenges.

However, once at the Spiritualist Association of Gt Britain, I had willingly allowed a test of my mediumship to take place. I had been asked to work with an unknown audience, who would be seated in a different room to myself. When I linked with Spirit and obtained the evidence of survival for people in this adjacent room, I proved that walls do not divide us from the spirit world.

Another time I worked with that fine teacher and medium Eileen Roberts, currently president of the Institute of Spiritualist Mediums. Again, my link was at a distance, somewhat further than a nearby room, and again the proof of survival was given. Eileen was the adjudicator...and she is not a person who is easily satisfied.

Challenges accepted for financial gain are not why I trained as a medium. That sort of thing always smacks of music hall stuff, not serious mediumship so I never accepted any of the challenges.

When you have mixed with as many of the well known names as I have, there will always be some suspicion that I could have known.

Just one example of this was when I worked at Croydon. Kenneth Lester Boddington returned to give his full name, which, of course, I might have known. But he then went on to give both his mother's and father's full names, his squadron number, date of passing and the address of his parents. It was a warm, human message during which he teased both parents about personal matters.

Some people have been kind enough over the years to follow through on messages. So many say that the recipient is known or it is faked, but so few take the trouble to check messages' accuracy. I cannot because I am usually going on to yet another town, another meeting.

One who did check up was Mrs Bain, then secretary of Newcastle-upon-Tyne's Spiritual Evidence Society which organised a meeting at the City Hall where Coral Polge worked with me. One recipient checked was Annie Thompson.

Mrs Thompson told Mrs Bain she had been told clairaudiently that morning that would receive a message. She was the first recipient. The drawing was of her mother, but looking much younger than when she left this earth plane. I told Mrs Thompson that. She agreed it was her mother at the age of 18.

There was a good reason for the age difference. Mrs Thompson had lost the only early photograph she had of her mother — and the drawing was a replica. I know how happy she was that Coral had been able to replace this treasured possession. Mrs Bain also checked upon the others...and all agreed that every detail was 100 per cent correct. Coral and I have worked many times together. I have a great respect for the work she has done, and she has for me.

With the training I received in my earlier days, the example of all the great mediums, including my mother with whom I worked, the endless examples of irrefutable evidence I have given to thousands of people all over the world means I have no need to manufacture anything. The facts that Spirit pass to others through my mediumship could not be equalled by anything from earthly origin.

It is a sad thing when Spiritualists quarrel, when their trust is tested and fails the test. In my position, I have been held responsible many times to uphold the integrity of our movement. Sometimes I have had to be there when other mediums are accused of fraudulent acts. I always try to keep in mind their feelings; I try not to judge harshly or even to judge at all.

There are people who think it is clever to try to trick mediums. Fortunately these are fewer in number now, but I imagine it still happens from time to time. For a while, a national paper tried this in order to manufacture stories. One quite well known paper sent a person to several mediums. They deliberately fed or indicated wrong things and were then surprised when they did not get a good reading.

Of course, any accusation of trickery on the part of a medium is always taken very seriously because we have a duty to police our own workers. We do not have a solid reputation in the world yet. This is one of the reasons why we have to be so careful, why any enquiry which is convened must be done to the rules.

We also have a duty to our mediums to make certain that any accusation has a solid foundation. Some people hear what they want to hear. Some cannot hear what is the truth. Mistakes can be made, and that must be kept in mind. We must uphold the integrity of Spirit and make certain that integrity is reflected in our own work.

I remember one lady's indignant letter in the paper defending mediums. It was from a Louis d'Amiens, who wrote: "Do not worry about the odd fake medium. If a bank clerk absconds with the cash do I lose faith in banking?" Perhaps not quite the right sentiments when applied to mediums. But her heart was in the right place even if her logic was not quite right.

Funnily enough, one of the nationals, the "Sunday Mirror," printed a tribute to my mediumship. It was a letter from Mrs E Pawlack of Huddersfield who attended a meeting, but did not stand up to identify her returned son. She stated, "He (Gordon Higginson) described how my son died and where he was buried." She confirmed that the details I had given were absolutely correct. There was also the testimony of a police radio technician who testified to his grandmother's materialisation. He confirmed, "She (the spirit form) had the right accent with a peculiar sibilance in speech and a characteristic stoop." This man was an Elder of the Church of Scotland.

We do face trials and tribulations as mediums, but so often ordinary people stand up when you are least expecting it and speak upon your behalf. Then, somehow, the hurt is eased a little. Thank God for the ordinary people of this world.

Chapter 22

MOTHER RETURNS

THERE were two people who were in my life. When these passed into Spirit I felt a great loss. One was, of course, my mother. She understood me, probably far more than I understood myself: she had cared for me, defended me and guided me through my life.

I realised when she was not there just how much I missed her and how much she had meant to me. When she passed away, I endeavoured to make contact with her, and asked to represent me, my sister and my niece, who has lived with me all her life.

I knew that if my mother was to return, it would be through this contact. I could have asked for a sitting for myself, but was so very well known as was my mother. It was for this reason that I asked people who would not be recognised to stand in my place. I wanted to be absolutely sure, you see.

Doris Stokes was visiting my church for the first time. I asked her to come to my house to give readings for some people. My niece left the house before she arrived so that Doris would not connect her with me.

After Doris arrived, I showed her into my dining room, where she was to work. When my sister arrived, I introduced her to Mrs Stokes. It was not an excellent sitting because there was a lot that could not be understood, but my sister did say she felt that Mother was trying to make contact, although she had not received any real evidence.

I told Mrs Stokes afterwards, of course, that she was my sister, explaining there was no intention of trickery: it was just that so many things were known about Mother and me.

I had also invited several complete strangers so that Mrs Stokes would not think it was just my family. After my niece had been in she felt that outstanding evidence had not been given. Mrs Stokes had done her best, but we could not be entirely satisfied. I suppose you could accept she had Mother there, but, as I say, I was not really happy.

I know I was very demanding in this because, perhaps, it was so very important to me. The evidence had to be absolute really.

We did not give up hope. I received so many phone calls and letters saying that Mother had communicated, but there was nothing I could say was unknown to others and so could not accept that the evidence I required had been given, some which would stand the test.

One day I decided to visit the cemetery where my mother was buried. I wondered if I visited that she might come through. I am not one to visit cemeteries because I know that only the body is there. But it seemed right at that time to make this pilgrimage, just to have a look at her last resting place on the earth.

I did not take a bunch of flowers, but a bud from a rose tree in our garden which I knew Mother loved. I stood at the end of the grave and spoke to her, saying: "Now come along, Mother. Aren't you concerned? Don't you want to speak to us and tell us what you are doing? What about telling us? We are all in need of a comfort from you. We miss you!"

I heard nothing. All was silent. I admit to looking around to make sure nobody was near enough to see my lips moving as I spoke to Mother. I said to her, in the normal way that a son would speak to his mother: "Now I think it is time you got up. I think you have slept too long."

It was partly in jest. I couldn't see my mother actually sleeping her way through eternity, but wanted her to know how much I was waiting, anxious to hear from her.

I thought little more about this incident for in spite of my natural grief I was very busy. Work goes on, as does life. I knew Mother would let us know in her own time that she had survived and that she liked where she was.

I went to Hyde church in Cheshire and I have wonderful memories of this church because Mr and Mrs Hyde, the president and secretary, are personal friends of mine. I have known them for many years. Indeed, when I visited them it was like a second home to me. They knew many of my friends and family.

I had promised to do a series of lectures and demonstrations.

They were the trustees of their church, which was always full when I visited. I was to be there for some five weeks.

The first evening a young woman came up to me and said she had been to a meeting of mine and, although very impressed, was not fully convinced. She had come deliberately to see me, and was booked for all five lectures and demonstrations.

"I am not a Spiritualist," the woman explained, "but an artist. I draw portraits and have done one of you." Well, when I looked, it was quite excellent. She had made me look young and handsome. I felt quite flattered at the likeness. "This is better than any photograph," I said when thanking her. The artist said she would like to do one every week "you are here for your face changes so much with each different expression."

For four weeks I was given a superb drawing of myself in different poses and was, naturally, very pleased with this. The woman was still not convinced, but was very interested. On the last night I was demonstrating and going through the various stages of development with the students.

I noticed that each time I looked at this young lady she was throwing all the papers on to the floor. I wondered why. She seemed irritated, frustrated with her work.

At the end of the evening, she said to me: "You know, Mr Higginson, I had thought this last portrait would be the best, but I couldn't get you at all. Every time I tried to draw you, you have turned out to be a lady. She is not even particularly like you, and wears glasses. I have given up!

"As you know," she added, "I am not even a Spiritualist. But as I was drawing I thought I heard a voice saying: 'Don't draw him dear. Draw me'." The young woman went on to say she had thought this was her imagination. I said for her not to worry because she had given me four excellent drawings and I was very happy with these.

I went to have a cup of tea with a friend, Ray Williamson. I said to him: "You know Ray, I can't help thinking about what that young lady said. I keep thinking that it sounds just like my mother. She would say that sort of thing. It's funny, but she keeps coming into my mind."

"Yes," said Ray, "but she said the woman wore glasses and

your mother didn't." Well, my mother didn't wear glasses in public, but she did at home when reading. Very few people ever saw her wearing glasses. There was certainly no published picture of her with glasses.

An incident occurred before her death which involved her wanting a new pair of glasses. I said to Mother that she couldn't have another pair because she already had several and never used them. In the end, I gave in because my mother was a very determined woman.

I arranged for a friend to come and bring some frames. I chose a pair I thought suitable for her years. She was 88 years old and these were quite suitable for that age. Mother refused: she wanted something a bit fancy so he went away and came back later with a different selection.

Mother ended up choosing a pair with diamantes, like glittery bits on the frame. My sister and I smiled. They were very fancy! We didn't think Mother would like those, but she did. I would have expected to see these on a young girl and laughed. Mother was put out. "I like these frames," she said. "I want these and am going to wear them."

Well, she didn't, not in this world. All these memories flooded back to me as I spoke to Ray. I rushed to the artist, begging her to give me the drawing of the lady wearing the glasses. Lo and behold! There was the most wonderful picture of my mother. There is no other like it in the world. Any other that has ever been printed is completely different to this likeness of mother.

This girl was not a Spiritualist, not mediumistic. Deep down she did not even really believe for she had received no personal proof for herself, not even from me — and said so! Nevertheless, there on paper was my mother's likeness with the self-same pair of glasses which she had sworn she would wear!

I was shaken rigid. I was in a town far away from where I live. This girl had no reason to know that my mother had passed. Only five or six people had ever seen Mother in glasses. It was the most wonderful proof for me.

I believe Mother did hear me when I asked her to make her return. She showed herself in her own way; it was so characteristic of her personality to do things in this way; so typical of her to say:

"Don't draw him dear. Draw me!"

Here was a living experience of someone's return. Mother, of all people, understood me. She knew the doubts I would have where other mediums might know of her and her life. Here was someone, an artist who had no such knowledge. I had to wait for the right person at the right time before I was to have this wonderful proof of my mother's survival.

Another important person in my life was Frank Tams, who was like a brother to me. I knew him from school-days. Frank was a very great friend through all the years. I think, apart from my mother, his loss into the spirit world was the greatest grief I had to bear.

Frank was my partner. He shared my business life and through this made it possible for me to travel in the ways I had to do to fulfil my work for the Spirit.

He helped me with my development. In many ways, Frank was my greatest critic. It is important for a medium to have someone to criticise, in a constructive fashion, the work they do. We cannot always be the best judge of our work because we are too close. We do the best that we can. Sometimes another person can look at it objectively and see things that need to be altered or improved.

Frank often took me around. He respected — perhaps even loved — me as a medium. I think that is why I am able to respect and to love other mediums and to help them in their work for I was given that support from Frank.

He was a comrade, a pal, someone who was always there. Scrupulously honest, Frank would never tell me I was good if I wasn't, but he didn't judge. He cared, you see.

When his passing came, it was so very hard for me. Frank did most of the work in our business to give me time for my work as a medium and within the union administration as president.

He was vice-president of Longton church where I have been the president for so many years. When I was not there, he took my place. Frank kept discipline, seeing to the everyday matters of running a church which can be so time consuming and are often onerous responsibilities. He was greatly loved by our members.

My family, my friends, the members of our church: we all felt his loss. Frank's passing was very sudden. He was at a Council meeting at Stansted Hall. Perhaps that is why Stansted has yet another memory for me for it was there, in the library, that he was called back to the spirit world.

Frank loved Stansted. We shared many happy hours there. Frank had just spoken. These are his last words spoken upon the earth within his physical body: "There are three loves in my life. The first is Longton Spiritualist Church, the second is Stansted Hall and the third is the Spiritualists' National Union. These are the three loves in my life." He sat down — and died.

I am lucky for those words were recorded so I have them on tape. I have often listened to it as I was not with him when he passed. I had not attended that Council meeting, but have his words.

It has been a call for me, almost as if he was saying: "Longton church is where you belong. Stansted Hall is a love. The union has your loyalty." His feelings in these things are mine. We shared so much, including many friends.

When they turned up at the funeral, I know he was there and would have been proud that so many cared to come. Our church had over two hundred people packed in — and there were more than one hundred in the large school room below. Even so there were well over another hundred people who could not get in, but stood outside.

I was very perturbed about Frank's passing. Why had I not been made aware of this imminent event which would make so much difference in my life? There I found that with these things it is very often better not to know. If you do, you have an expectancy and that is conveyed no matter how hard you try, no matter how well you control your feelings.

So I felt that perhaps all that happened was for the best. The night before I had taken the service at Sutton Coldfield, a special one of re-dedication. I had asked for instructions to get the right road to Stansted for I should have been at the Council meeting.

I got on to the motorway at the wrong junction. Indeed, I was going in the wrong direction and was travelling north instead of south. After about half an hour I realised. By the time I could turn back, I was nearer my home than the hall, and decided to sleep in my own bed and to get up early.

The next day, instead of getting up in time to travel south to Stansted which is quite a long way from Longton, I overslept. The telephone call from there came for me before I could phone them. I did not travel south, but gave my apologies; I would not attempt to attend the remainder of the meeting.

I was devastated, but had no time to express my grief for that night I was due to take a special meeting at Hanley. I feel that Spirit had not intended me to be there to see my old friend move beyond the veil for if I had I might not have been able to contain my sorrow.

Over 1,500 people had already bought tickets for the Town Hall in Hanley. Tom Johanson, the great spirit healer, was booked. His wife, Coral Polge that wonderful medium and psychic artist, was to work with me. The meeting was a fantastic success.

Coral has since said she felt as if we were floating through time and space. I told no-one about Frank except Tom and Coral until after the service. The choir from our church were there. Many in the audience also knew Frank; I didn't want them to know until afterwards.

I managed to give what Coral has described as an "astounding demonstration of clairvoyance." I know my friend would have wanted it that way. We shared a common goal. Frank had devoted his life, as I had mine, to proving the continuance of life after death.

Here was I at a time when I had to find that great strength as a medium so as to carry on. It was only at the end of the meeting when my mother, who had travelled to be near me, took my hand that I was able to give way.

Oddly enough, I have had portraits of Frank given to me indirectly, drawn for another, but intended for me. Again, so many people knew of my close contact with Frank that perhaps this was the best way for him to send me a keepsake from his new life.

Of course, there have been times when I would have enjoyed a normal home-life with a companion to share the warmth of the fire and the problems of living.

I have been lucky in many ways. Apart from the unique help and friendship I shared with my partner and childhood friend Frank Tams, there is one other to whom I have owed so very much. Again, he is a fellow speaker and worker for Spirit within the union. I refer to Eric Hatton, who has been more than a friend to me. He and his wife, Heather, have been a second family.

Eric was ordained by me in April 1977 at his own church in Stourbridge, where he had then been president for nearly 20 years. He chose Albert Taylor to be his sponsor. Albert was 90 then and had worked for Stourbridge for 60 years. Laura, Eric's sister, wrote a hymn for the occasion. They are a very musical family. Eric has won prizes for singing, and has the most marvellous tenor voice.

Eric never wanted to be a Spiritualist. It was his family who were the influence after they became interested. Eric argued for ages before he decided to investigate for himself. Then he had wonderful evidence which finally convinced him.

Eric's brother was killed at Singapore on what would have been his last flight in the RAF. Eric received a letter which said his brother had communicated at a seance. The medium gave his name, nickname, his RAF number and numerous other details, all of which were absolutely correct.

While still in the Forces, Eric had healing from Harry Edwards which was so successful that he did not need a second scheduled operation on his spine. Later, he found out that his partner in business was a Spiritualist. Then he married Heather, who was a clairvoyant. Eric was obviously destined to be a Spiritualist and has done some marvellous work in the movement. He has been one of my closest friends and most staunch supporter.

So many dear friends have moved on beyond the veil, but these two very dear friends are still with us, still working hard on behalf of Spirit, their church and the union. I knew Eric and Heather Hatton before they were married, and was the medium responsible for giving Eric and his sister the evidence which brought them into the movement. It was at Birmingham Town Hall when his brother, was a pilot, returned to speak to his sister.

At that time they had no idea of whether he was alive or not. The brother had been reported missing, presumed killed. He could have been a prisoner. They just did not know — until that night!

Eric has spoken to me of this since and reminded me how I gave his brother's name, his service number and other details. Even Eric didn't know whether the number I supplied that night was correct. They had to check it out.

It was from that meeting that I came to know this man. In all these years we have not fallen out. We have not always agreed because he is a man who will not relinquish what he believes just for the sake of friendship. Eric has an integrity, which is a wonderful thing.

He does not just work in administration. Eric is a first class speaker, a wonderful healing channel for Spirit and one of our leading ministers. He is so gentle and yet has a strength of purpose and a natural dignity which upholds the very meaning of Spiritualism.

I think that my friendship with Eric and his lovely wife has been one of the most important that I have had in my life. I treasure this friendship deeply. They are great Spiritualists. Their home has been a second home to me.

When, in 1990, I had several strokes which left me very weak and vulnerable, they took me, cared for me and helped to bring me back to good health. Without their nursing and care, which took all the weight from me, I do not know what would have happened.

Heather put me on a strict diet of balanced food and tender loving care, which speeded my recovery. Eric took on all my duties as president as well as carrying out his own as vice-president. All this was in spite of his own health problems and business responsibilities. No one could wish for a better friend or co-worker. I love them both.

In my work as a medium, Eric has helped me. I am only sorry he has never felt that, because of his work, he could take on the presidency because I am convinced he would be a wonderful president.

I knew and loved his mother and father. His mother, I felt, was a giant among women. She was small and thin, but had so much love. It was my privilege to bring her lost son back to communicate with his family, such a small return for that which has been given to me over these years by these wonderful people.

Chapter 23

SPIRITUALISM SHOWS THE WAY

I BELIEVE that Spiritualism is the oldest known movement in the world. There has always been a Spiritualism, not as we understand it today, but never the less contact with the higher forces of the spirit world, going as far back as Abraham. He was a medium, a prophet, a seer, chosen to do the work of Spirit because the Lord, Yaweh, spoke to him.

Abraham was given directions of how to lead his people. He heard voices and saw angels as did so many in both the Old and, to some extent, the New Testament. Mohammed had visions. He too heard voices; he hid under a cloak or went into a dark cave. The Patriarchs entered the Inner Temple whilst the disciples with Jesus went up at dusk into lonely places. Unless you think of Spiritualism and experience Spiritualism, you cannot understand the old religions. They are full and rich with spiritual experiences as known and understood by Spiritualists.

In the past, mediums were burned at the stake and persecuted because priests wanted to suppress the truth. They wanted people to believe in a heaven with pearly gates and clouds, harps and all such things. The priests spread the word about a hell, where, if you didn't obey certain rules, you would suffer through fire and brimstone. Such silly ideas!

All that has been cleared away because the knowledge of Spiritualism has brought an understanding of truth into today's minds and a recognition of how things really are.

The two most wonderful experiences of anyone's life are birth and death. The soul is born to this earth to find individuality and personality. The real you is not what is seen in the mirror, but what is inside of the body, the self. You are born here and will live here. You will not die because there is no death. You are spirit and mind first and body second so it behoves you to learn as much as possible about your real self in the meantime.

Modern Spiritualism began in 1848 by a spirit visitation to two girls, the Fox sisters, and the hearing of knocks and raps. It took the girls to bring an organisation into these things. They devised a formula, a code, and received answers to their questions. It was a very simple method of communication with this invisible form: one for "No," two for "Yes" and three for doubtful.

Through this simple way, they were able to communicate with another mind, a person, who once had lived upon the earth. Indeed, he was murdered in the very house in which the girls lived. Later, the body was found to prove the truth of what had been said.

A lot has been written about the retraction which was later made by one of the sisters. She subsequently admitted she had been paid for this and needed the money. The girls were very human and had weaknesses. Isn't it marvellous that Spirit should choose such ordinary people, like you and me, with human failings, to bring about this revelation? After all, the disciples of Jesus were very simple fishermen, with human failures and weaknesses. Judas betrayed Jesus for 30 pieces of silver.

The Hydesville rappings, as this phenomenon became known, was a very different form of communication from that which has been given through the centuries. It was a very necessary breakthrough from the spirit world. Throughout history the power of the Spirit has made similar breakthrough at times when the world needed it most. In all religions there is truth. None has all the truth. Spiritualism has many beams of light, but not all the light.

I am quite sure that in the highways and byways of life there were individuals before the Fox sisters who had the imagination and intelligence to devise a reciprocal code of communication, but it was at this point in history that the explosion of publicity towards "Is there life after death?" was made.

I believe that the life of Jesus came about 2,000 years ago to give hope to those who had given it up; to free those who lived in virtual slavery; to help them to evolve on to higher spiritual levels upon the earth.

Likewise, I believe the world today needs the message

Spiritualism can offer. Spiritualism began in the simple way with simple folk as did the message of Jesus and all the great past Masters. These raps may have been a crude way, but was it not because of its simplicity that notice was taken and so many people began to believe in it?

The idea of Spiritualism is to unite nations together, not to divide them. Spiritualism is about life, not death. It is not a religion that forces itself upon you, which tells you that you cannot do this and you cannot do that, or unless you do this or do that you cannot survive. Survival does not depend upon your religion or what teacher you follow. Similarly, survival does not depend upon whether you are a saint or a sinner, an atheist or Christian, a Jew, Muslim or Buddhist.

It makes no difference. Your heaven will be what you have made of it. You can only reap what you have sown. Spiritualism gives the key to life as no other movement can. It shows you the way.

Spiritualism tells you that God is not a man or a woman. God is power and influence in the world, an invincible power which in the beginning created the whole. There is a great mind of which we know so little about, a mind that knows no creed, no dogma.

We do not need anyone to intercede for us with God. We teach people to go to God alone. It is their God equally with priests, ministers or whoever their mentor may be. Each person can move towards this power. The body is the temple of the spirit. The Spirit abides within you. It is part of the creative force itself.

Today we live in what men choose to call a practical age. Few pause to consider that the every day wonders of our time are but the crystalised dreams of yesterday.

Our pioneers searched the heavens. They refused to accept that in the sweet bye and bye we would meet on some distant shore. They wanted evidence now to convince them to live their life according to the laws of God.

They searched and found their loved ones on the highway of eternity, waiting for them. They could not come to us until we would accept them. They had tried, but always been turned away because we had been taught that to communicate with the dead is evil.

We found that our loved ones had long persevered to make that contact, but those they wished to greet were afraid of the damnation promised to those who drew aside the veil. The Church had promoted that fear for their own ends. But in the end, the truth had to be shown.

Through the two girls who devised their code to speak with the spirit world, the era of superstition drew to its end. Can anyone honestly believe that it was coincidence? The thread of God's power through His ministering angels is strong and bright.

The channels that could enlighten mankind as never before were found. The love that never dies was manifest again, here upon the earth. If Spiritualism has done just one thing it is that it has made heaven not a place, but a state of consciousness.

People are listening. Young people want to know and need to learn. I believe that those from the branches of the Christian faith who have done everything they can to stop us have done an eternal wrong, a wrong to the myriad of people who have passed over to the spirit world where they found the truth out for themselves. These people could have saved themselves tremendous anxiety and concern for their awakening into the other world was something they feared.

They had been taught to fear the unknown, to fear all things to do with the eternal life, to fear God! Oh how sad, how very sad, to think of all those souls approaching that moment of transition in dread instead of the joy that we know to be their right. To fear the wrath of God instead of looking for the light of His countenance.

Spiritualism has cleared all that for so many who have listened to the truth. The love and beauty of God is revealed.

I remember listening to a most moving and wonderful lecture when I was a young man. I cannot now remember the name of the orator, but his words have stayed with me. He said that the new age had opened up for him the realisation that God was on the move. I believe that God has been on the move for several centuries now, trying to bring us forward into the light of truth.

We must move away from old ideas such as leaving the dead alone. How can we leave the dead when we have proved there are no dead? How can we leave those who love us, whose only fault is that they no longer have a body?

Those who have passed have gone beyond that untruth and know that they still live. It is only the physical which dies since the soul continues to exist and live. That is where love is such a powerful experience. It is love that breaks through the barriers, that tears the veil from the eye of the earthly body.

It is wrong of anyone to condemn those things about Spiritualism without reason, without fact, and very often without knowledge.

Some have claimed that investigation into Spiritualism sends people mad, and fills asylums. Papers tried to prove this — only to find that there are more from other religions who suffer in this way!

My experience of Spiritualism has been that it has prevented, not caused, harm. It has helped; it restores faith and gives access to truth. I have often found that knowledge of Spiritualism has actually helped those from other religions to understand their own traditions more clearly.

So many see only what they want to see, closing their ears to those things they do not want to know. They exist within their narrow frame and ignore the extent of God's power and wisdom.

We must get rid of this idea that heaven is a place or hell is a place. We must teach that these are levels of consciousness. We must get a clear interpretation of what the afterlife is like to help more people to get rid of their fears so they can live good lives. It is so important we remember that we are spirit now.

So often we speak of spirit people "coming back." They don't go anywhere; they don't come back from anywhere. They are here all around us, but in another dimension. People still think of God as being "Up there" in heaven and hell as being "Down there." Well, of course, we know that isn't really true, but we have to educate our children to what really is true.

The events in the Spiritualist movement are the most important religious happenings for two hundred years. Sir Arthur Conan Doyle wrote: "The dawn is breaking. The greatest revelation to mankind has been made. All that is wanted is that mankind should understand that revelation...When I read the New Testament with the knowledge I have of Spiritualism I am led to the deep conviction that the teaching of Christ was lost, in many important respects, by the old church and has not come down to us."

Bernard Shaw was another remarkable man. He wrote: "I am a medium. When I take my pen or sit down to my typewriter, I am as much a medium as Daniel Dunglas Home or as Joan of Arc."

The spirit writings of the Christian and many great religions are declared by their sects to be the word of God. Yet the spirit writings of Spiritualism are deemed to be from the subconscious or imagination. I do not see the difference.

I do not give all credence to any writing just because it is declared to be on behalf of something in which I believe. Many of the so-called spirit writings produced in the name of Spiritualism have within them as many faults and mis-statements as those of old which are venerated because of their stated source rather than their rational content.

We cannot, should not, reduce everything to the rational, but we must apply a certain logic when assessing the work of any medium, be they from ancient times or from this era.

We have discovered a world within this one. The more we explore this, the closer it comes. We speak of our loved ones in the past. In our mind we confine them to the past. All this must go for we know that they live on and can come close to us here and now. They are not in the past unless we think them to be gone.

Jesus told us quite absolutely what the next world was all about, saying, "Where I am going, you, too, will come." He didn't say that when we go there we will wait until the last day. That has been put in since. Jesus also said he was going to prepare a place for us, and that we will do even greater things than he did. He told people to go out and do it. Then along came the Church, which decided it knew better and that people should not do the things he did! It doesn't make sense; what we teach must make sense.

We have to look at things in depth. We mustn't teach things unless they can be proved to be true. We teach people to look at things themselves, as Sir Arthur Conan Doyle and so many others looked for themselves. Then it will make sense to you — and you will be able to use these truths in your life.

What will we find? That God is not a man, that God is not a Judge, that we will not rise when the last trumpet sounds, but that there is a continuation of life. Our message is simple: there *is* a continuity of life after death.

I know there are some who say that Jesus was a God, and Sai Baba is a God, but I think we exceed our capabilities to try and personalise God in this way. We can't do that because if we do, we are putting it into a state where we must then say, "Well, who was responsible for God?" Then we will get entirely confused.

With all religious philosophies there are areas which cannot be explained. Most say they have explained and that which has no rational explanation must be taken on faith. At least Spiritualists have some sense and realise there are many things which cannot be understood by the earth mind. The earth mind simply does not have the points of reference necessary to understand all the wonders.

What we have to try and understand and accept is that there is this wonderful power of love, and that as we make progress so we will understand more about this power.

What we do know is that we are spiritual beings in a body. The evidences support that as a fact through all the ages. All the great philosophers and teachers came to this conclusion. I always remind people of Socrates because I believe him to be one of the great ones of all time.

Socrates lived well before Jesus and knew about life after death. He said quite definitely, "Don't tell the people when you bury me that you are burying Socrates." He knew, you see, that he was going on; that his body would be there, but he would not be.

Socrates did not adhere to his society's religious practices; that was part of his problems. But he saw things clearly and was not afraid to speak out in truth, his truth. It was right for him so he did not fear life or death. Socrates was not frightened to leave the physical life. Somehow, he knew he was moving forward, not coming to an end.

When you leave your body, it is like taking off your clothes and putting on a different suit. It is as easy as that! You will not get the best out of Spiritualism unless you change mentally. If you stay the same as you were and believe all the old theories about coming back in the body and things like that, you are best staying with your old religion. Religion is no use to you unless you can take from it the things that you need; not necessarily want, but need.

In religion, you must remain where your heart is. There should be no argument between religions, certainly not with the

Spiritualist. I don't think that it is the right religion for everybody.

I was once associated with some people when I was a young man; some very good friends. One was a very nice young lady whom I met during the war in Greece whilst the other was a young man. He and I just seemed to understand each other. Even our thoughts were the same. He actually came to me, just after he was killed.

At that time, I could not help thinking and wondering what God was doing. I too had to question "How can there be a God? How can there be this supreme power who gives and then, all at once, takes everything so drastically and so dreadfully?"

After the war I was going to return to Greece to visit my other friend and meet her family. Then I received news that she had been killed very tragically. "Why?" I wondered "Why has this happened?" There were many people whom I knew during the war who were slaughtered. All over the world at that time whole families had been wiped out.

I was shaken very deeply by her death and had to sit down. Even as Spiritualists we are shaken by dreadful events. We have souls; we have feelings; we have thoughts.

At that point, I could not see any future. I felt that if this is what it was all about, there must be something missing, something very wrong.

The answer comes within our movement and with experience. Sometimes, as young people we have not yet taken our religion to our heart as we should have done. Very often in the early stages we are taken with the wonders of it and with the evidence.

When the point comes and strikes your very heart and soul, it happens to you. You are shaken for a while, Then comes the time when you "know." Unless you have given serious thought to the evidences given, you could easily turn from the knowledge of God and Spiritualism.

Perhaps when this happens you will find out that you are not ready for Spiritualism yet. Spiritualism is the greatest challenge to life. There will be tests — and this is right. We must face the most serious questions about God and life.

If you have taken your religion seriously and learned about more than those things of the present, more than just the surface, then you will meet the challenge, face the test and emerge from sorrow and pain a stronger person, a stronger spirit.

The first thing that comes to me when I think of Spiritualism — and people think I am rather crazy when I say this — is that I am rather fond of funerals. I quite like the marriage service, but sometimes wonder how long it will last: the marriage, that is. Sometimes with naming services I worry a little for the future of the spirit I am holding in my arms. But with funerals I know that all is well!

I know through my experience of taking these services that I can talk to those who have just passed and that they are quite safe. I also know they will come and thank me for taking their service.

Of course, I cannot always tell the family because they are in the midst of their grief still, but the departed are with me. The words I speak are with the mourner, but my thoughts are with the departed. That is such a good feeling because they will then go on to their new life.

This wonderful knowledge has helped me to come to terms with the disasters and the sadness of losing a loved one from the earth.

Spiritualists do not have a special knowledge of why their loved ones are taken at the time of parting. They have the knowledge of continuous life. The Spiritualist does at least know that no life is wasted, no experience is wasted, although we cannot see the whole pattern.

Concerning prayer, I have often said that the training of mediums should not include instructing them how to pray. I stand by that. By the time a person is entitled to describe him or herself as a potential medium, they should have a knowledge of what prayer is.

You see, I believe that prayer is important in our lives, perhaps the most important part of our development. It has such powerful implications, it can have such an effect upon us. It is no use developing the psychic unless you have also learned about yourself as a spirit being, a part of God.

When you pray, you become the prayer. We understand that God is an inner power, not outside at all. When you ask for something in prayer, it is no use expecting an outside power to come along and give you what you have requested. But if you recognise that and can become your prayer through the sincerity and depth of your thoughts, then you have the answer.

God has to find the ways and the means whereby your prayer can be answered. How does that happen? Well, we have, through prayer and intention, opened the doors to the spirit world, bringing this other world close. Instead of being "Up there" a million miles away, we have brought it here, close to us.

We have discovered a world that is ours. We belong there; we have rights which are waiting to be claimed. The more we explore this, the closer it comes.

Given that we accept there is no God as a personality, why do we pray? Who is going to hear us? Surely it is our loved ones, those who are closest to us who will hear us. Those who have been given spiritual charge of our welfare upon the earth.

Here in Spiritualism we often call these guides or helpers. Very often it is these who put thoughts into our minds for our moral and spiritual development. It is important that we learn to listen to these.

Prayer is not all about asking, demanding even, when we think that we are asking for the right things. Prayer is listening, communicating, being at one with reality; the reality of God.

In prayer, we become our God. And if we listen, we are given the answers, the strength and knowledge to see through our troubles, not from an outside source, but from our inner reality

In that touching of our soul with the Great Soul of the Universe, we are filled with love and humility. We no longer want for ourselves, but that which is right for humanity.

It may be that we have our part to play. Then we will be given the strength of purpose to fulfil our task. It might be that we have to stand back and allow events to shape our lives so we are given the understanding which helps us to do this.

It can take many years to learn to pray properly. Some will never learn. But all the time we have to try. Of course, the more we try, the better we get.

I have sometimes been filled with the most complete feeling of love and belonging through prayer. Then I know I am in touch. When I thank God for all that I have, I am reminded of that which has been given to me. When I give thanks, I am reminded forcibly of the beauty of the universe and I am with God.

I always think that part of our prayers should be an acknowledgement of the closeness of the spirit world, not because my friends in that world need to be reminded, but I, as a human soul, need to be reminded of that love which is given so freely from those realms.

Each person will experience prayer in their own way because each of us is different. There are some who will use a formula, but I do not think that this has great value.

When you use the same words over and over, they become at best not a prayer but a mantra, and that is a different matter entirely. Prayer must be stimulated from the heart, not the memory.

Each medium who works upon the platform will have to know how to pray for the sake of others. Their own prayers will be very different in content than those they express in public.

Prayer crystalises within you what you are feeling about yourself, about your fellow man and about your God. It is an expression of where you are and what you are.

If you have absorbed the love of God and Spirit, this will be manifest in your prayer. If you have a sincere desire to help and to make progress in your own progress, this will be heard by those near to you.

You will become the instrument of your desires through the help of the spirit world. All too often the effect of the subconscious mind is under-estimated. We have all that is needed within us. Prayer can free us from the limitations we place upon ourselves.

Chapter 24

APPARITIONS

THERE seems to be an upsurge in interest in ghosts and such things these days. Fundamentalist Christians, for instance, appear to concentrate on evil things. They talk glibly about possession and obsession, but really seem to know very little about the things they are dealing with.

I think this is very dangerous because they are putting all sorts of thoughts into people's minds and seem to be directing them to devil worship and child abuse. I admit that I just cannot fathom out what their true purpose is.

What worries me is that I believe that thoughts shape what we are. If we pray and think of good, positive things, we are far more likely to be positive and to lead a good life. We touch good and are influenced by that good.

What is happening around all these people who think so much of evil? We know that the monks who were obsessed with the "evils of the flesh" in the Middle Ages so shaped events that thousands of innocent people died and were tortured in the centuries of the inquisition.

Well, I am sure that this could not happen again, even if the Fundamentalists do sometimes seem to want it. It is their future I worry about. To be so immersed in thoughts of evil, the devil and sin? They must attract negative influences for like attracts like. I am concerned for the state of their souls.

Of course, it would be silly to ignore the fact that some spirit entities are disturbed, but generally they need help. That is what I have found over the years. Perhaps it is because Spiritualists do not think evil thoughts that evil is not attracted to them.

I think some people are starting to seek out more knowledge. They talk more about energies and residual memories, but very few actually approach us who do know about such things.

I have been involved in so many situations of helping both people and Spirit. Very few have been difficult. I read about "rescue circles" and often smile to myself.

Sometimes, I hear of someone who has only been in the movement a short time and who has had no training as a medium. They have little knowledge of Spirit, but announce to all who will listen that they sit in a rescue circle. Then I do get really worried. Most of these are harmless enough, but there are situations where they could get themselves into terrible difficulties.

I do wish that such people would use a little common sense. Someone who has not yet learned to swim would hardly take a position as a lifeguard and yet these people want to rescue spirit beings, knowing nothing of the conditions in the spirit world. Those who run circles where such people are sitting should know better, but obviously do not.

I do know I have been able to help many times and in many places either where Spirit is manifesting and needs help or where poltergeist activity is taking place and again my help has been needed. I know there are many other mediums who will undertake this work, although not all will do so.

Once, I remember, I was asked by a local firm to come and sort out a problem they were having with the appearance of one of their workers who should have been peacefully going about her business in the spirit world, but instead was making a bit of a nuisance of herself in her old work-place.

Many had given in their notice after seeing this "apparition" so the management were getting rather worried. Well, I went along and spoke to some of those who had seen this "ghost." They thought it was a man who had taken his own life.

I linked into the spirit world and was immediately aware of the presence of a woman. I described her. Several there were able to recognise her. Of course, it helped that I was able to give her name to them.

I spoke to her very nicely, asking her what she wanted. She wished to speak to a colleague who was working elsewhere in the pottery. She told me where to send for this friend. Doris was her name. Someone went off and fetched her.

It turned out that this poor soul had not been very happy at home, but lived for her work where she was happy. She wanted to thank her friend for her kindness, particularly on the last day of her earthly life when she had been taken ill and Doris took her home. She promised not to haunt there any more; all she wanted really was to pass on her thanks. She now felt free to go forward.

A Spiritualist would not think too much of this, but the work's manager was a sceptic and rather astounded. The press and radio made quite a thing of it for a while. I suppose the whole matter gave a few people food for thought.

Another time, I was able to help a family living at Bignall End who had been troubled by an apparition, being woken up every morning at 3 am in addition to hearing noises and seeing doors flying open on their own. Very naturally this family were in need of help...and sleep!

Through my mediumship, I was able to contact the departed entity and find out what was wrong, what was troubling her. It was an earthly matter, a problem about a will in fact, but she still worried about it. This was quite silly in itself, but troubled her mind even in the spirit world.

I was able to let the family know about this. I don't think anything could be done to rectify the matter, but the spirit of the departed was apparently satisfied at having made a point.

It was a very interesting case, and highlights the fact that most "hauntings" are caused by very mundane matters. If these causes are discovered, then the matter can be put right and the spirit being move forward to fulfil his or her spiritual destiny.

I am often quite appalled when I read or hear about the way "exorcisms" are carried out. I explained the Spiritualist attitude on BBC TV's "Nationwide." I tried to put over that props are quite unnecessary: all that was needed was a medium to communicate with the earthbound entity causing such disturbances.

For instance, priests or clergy use water during their ceremony. They say they exorcise the spirit by these means, but water can have no effect upon the spiritual! Why should the spirit world understand or be effected by a physical substance?

This is quite apart from that rather obvious fact these people seem to think that a communicating spirit is in the body when, of course, we know that the spirit draws close to the body within the auric field, but does not enter the physical body.

Spirit can effect control through the etheric, but are not in the body itself. These things must be explored further, but we do know this much.

Kindness and understanding go a long way when you are dealing with people, whether they are here on earth or in the world of Spirit. The wording of the service of exorcism is ancient and absolutely terrifying. It has none of the loving grace of God within it. How people who say they work for our loving Father can contemplate such a service, I fail to comprehend.

Not all my experiences with ghosts have been entirely serious. I remember one year. I think it must have been in the 1970s or thereabouts.

I was asked by a television company in Manchester to appear on a programme which was to be broadcast on Christmas morning. It planned to discuss with some other people the matter of haunted houses.

They couldn't tell me at that time just who else would be on the programme, but it was to be filmed in an old house on the Derbyshire Moors. I was quite delighted and agreed. I went off to buy a dinner jacket because we were to be at a dinner party and then all gathered round a fire during this discussion. We were to dress up.

I arrived at the inn where it had been arranged I would meet the others. I rather thought I was going to be the star, and still didn't know who else was to be there. I knocked upon the door as I could hear people talking inside.

As I opened the door and went in there was a silence. I heard someone say, "Good God!" I was a little taken aback since I looked quite respectable. "What is wrong?" I asked, thinking to myself, "Well, I can always go home."

"You look quite human," came the reply. "We were rather expecting someone quite different, you know, glaring eyes." People had some really odd ideas about Spiritualist mediums then, and even now!

We gathered around to hear what was expected of us. We were to be taken by coach to this old house. It was to seem as if we had lost our way in the mist and arrived by chance. The film crew were to supply the mist by means of a machine.

We set off all right, but nature supplied us with a much better fog than the film crew and we couldn't find the house! We had lost it. "Well," I thought, "this is a good start." But we carried on. We had no choice really because we were expected and everybody was waiting.

Eventually we arrived. It was not a house at all but an old ruined castle. We knocked at the door. I was thinking: "They will never make anything of this. It looks awful." A butler took us in and went in to this beautiful room. It had no roof except for a sort of cover the TV company put up, but looked wonderful. We had to wait for the next scene to be got ready. There was a wonderful chandelier. It really looked quite grand. As we sat there, the door opened. In came some workmen carrying a very large table.

"Is this all right, Mr Higginson? Will this do?" they said. I looked at it and said yes, it was very nice. I was a little bewildered, but it really was a very pleasant table. Little did I know that I was expected to levitate this enormous and weighty object in the course of the evening. It was just as well because I might have left there and then!

I had been joined by some very nice ladies, one of whom was to be my dinner partner, Professor Cohen from the Psychology Department of Manchester University and a Dr Barker, who was a psychiatrist. I thought the former would presumably be the opposing view and the latter deciding whether I was mad. It promised to be very interesting. They were very respected people, and good conversationalists.

We were to talk about the Grey Lady, apparitions and things like that. They rather thought that the Grey Lady would appear and I would be able to tell them about her. There was to be an interviewer who would keep the conversation moving and ask any questions.

The television programme would last a full hour, but I was aware, as were the others, that it would be the last five minutes, after the producer signalled, which would be remembered. We would all try for this spot as we all wanted to put our own point forward to be remembered.

The conversation was going well. Then my young lady put her hands onto the table top. "Oh," she said, "I am sure I can feel vibrations. Wouldn't it be wonderful if the table was to rise in the air?" "Yes," said I, looking thoughtfully at the size of the table. "It would be a miracle." I said this under my breath because I didn't want them to think I was being facetious.

Time passed. Everyone was wondering about the Grey Lady. They really thought she was going to appear for them and asked me. I wasn't aware of anyone around, and said so.

Towards the end of our time together the presenter of the programme started his signal. "Well," I immediately said, "Professor Cohen, may I ask you a question?" He had to say "Yes" and so I had the last five minutes.

I gave the professor a contact I had for him and a few details which I was given by this communicator. "Professor Cohen," said the interviewer. "Mr Higginson has given you some very good evidence to support what he has been saying here. Do you accept it?" "No," said Professor Cohen. "Why?" asked the interviewer. "I cannot accept it until my colleagues accept it" was the astounding reply.

It was not enough to prove to him: I would have to prove to all those of his faculty! Well, we can only keep on proving to the masses because with that attitude we will have difficulty in being accepted by those of the scientific fraternity. Anyway, it was a very nice evening. We did not see any ghost, but I am not even sure they had one there.

The media is like that. They want the dramatic. It is not enough to sit and discuss our standpoint, our philosophy. They want that which will amaze — and even then don't accept it.

The question very often arises, "What is the difference between ghost, poltergeist and spirit?"

I think confusion has arisen from the past when people would very often see a spirit form and call this a ghost. Any spirit form was classed as a ghost. In most circumstances, they mean exactly the same thing. But when you come to the word "poltergeist," there must be an understanding.

I have never believed in evil spirits. I accept that there are evil spirits, but don't believe they affect or interfere with life here.

I think that a great deal which is taken for poltergeist phenomena is that someone in the spirit world has powers which can be used to move objects and things of that sort.

It is not just things flying about or being moved, trumpets or tables being lifted: these are psychic phenomena. You can have these things without the power of the spirit world. When investigating anything like this, you have to be prepared to find out the mind that is behind it.

Very often, there is no mind behind it; very often when you get a haunted house a lot of the phenomena are unexplained. I have been to haunted houses and found no spirit entity, no apparent cause for the phenomena. I think there is a lot that we do not know. This is one thing that has not been fully explored.

It is like an energy. Sometimes the source of this energy can be found in children, usually adolescents. It is like a person who puts their hand on the table and find they can control it. Their own mind is the instrument of control, but if they don't know this, they will think it is from a Spirit source.

When the table is moved by Spirit or the phenomena are instigated by Spirit, there will be intelligence behind it. Very often those who are recounting "ghost" stories will exaggerate the feelings and impressions which they feel. This is probably not done deliberately, but in the mind the effect is enhanced by imagination and expectation.

I remember that in the story I recounted about the ghost in the factory so much had been exaggerated. People were feeling nooses about their neck and other weird experiences which simply had not happened. There was no doubt there was a spirit there, but she was quite benign and would not have promoted bad feelings. She was just lonely. After people realised this, there was no more problem.

In the genuine case, there is a feeling in the air, often as cold, but there is seldom any harm. It is from the past that people bring in ideas about the devil and evil and all sorts of things which simply are not present.

I remember some years ago in my church at Longton. I was a Lyceumist. Each year we used to go away together. One year a group went with Mrs Lloyd to Abergelly. We stayed at a house and had circles late at night.

One evening, we went out for a walk by the sea shore. I was conscious that there was someone with us. We spoke of this to Mrs Lloyd and agreed we should try and find out who this spirit was. I was a working medium at the time, although this was long ago, so it was agreed I should be the intermediary.

We found out that the person was a relative of the people who ran the house, a young lady. This young woman had gone out one night and never been seen since. The feeling I had when I first became aware of the entity was a very cold one, the sensation of a presence, not unpleasant and not strong enough for me to be able to identify there and then. It was only when we sat deliberately to try and make contact with this spirit that I was able to bring forward the memory of identity.

This coldness is not the same as the cold felt by normal atmospheric conditions; there is a difference which cannot be described in words and can only be identified through experience. We must get rid of the idea that these people lie down waiting for the revival of life.

Life goes on. Sometimes spirit beings do not move on into their new life, but are drawn to their familiar memories of earth. The sooner people realise that heaven is not Up There but is around us the better.

These spirits sometimes need some help to recognise that they no longer need to stay within the limitations of the human atmosphere. What angers me sometimes is the thought of priests and ministers deliberately trying to banish them from what is familiar without making any effort to show them the wonderful life they are missing. Spirit life is far less limited than our life here.

There are energies around us which are not personalised. This can have effect upon the earth and the things of earth. Sometimes that energy can cause destruction, but is no more evil than a hurricane.

We have a great deal to learn yet. Perhaps it is time that more serious efforts were made to investigate these matters. This has been done from the scientific viewpoint, using instruments to try and measure atmospheric changes.

It has been done as a research into who has seen an apparition, where, and when. It is time it was done from the positive knowledge of the Spiritualist, using any technology that would be of help, but keeping in mind that the genuine "ghost" is probably a departed spirit with something to say!

Chapter 25

THE MEDIA

WE have always had varied response from the media. Of course, at one time that just meant the papers or the radio. Some very early broadcasts were made, but we have no record of these for our archives.

Ernest Oaten actually made the very first broadcast talk on Spiritualism on Friday, April 13, 1934. He was at that time a member of the Council and also editor of "Two Worlds." I was a very young man then, just starting my career.

Ernest spoke of his youth and his first attendance at a seance in Cardiff in 1892, his subsequent experimentation and later experiences and conversion to Spiritualism. There was a pamphlet printed by the Two Worlds Publishing Company, but it has been out of print for many years now.

The response of the public was widespread. Hundreds of letters were received asking for further details. It is still quite amazing how people do respond to this exposure; it is also amazing how many know nothing about our movement. I think we must take advantage of opportunities, but must be careful.

I have often been interviewed for radio, but they seldom record our services. One time in Nottingham, though, in about 1980 we had a tremendous convention. Over 2,000 attended. It was held at the university. Spiritualist Muriel Turner arranged it as she was very good at organising. Two of our services there were recorded for Radio Trent.

The Great Hall was filled to capacity. I remember thinking what a pity that it wasn't televised because it would have looked very good. The sight of all those Spiritualists would have been marvellous to see.

Over the years I have had many invitations to appear on television, but I do not like the way they consider mediums. It is almost as if we are a peep show. I do not think that our work is taken seriously in the media. The problem is that the people filming the programme may well be very sincere, but the finished result does not always reflect well upon us as a movement.

What I have done is given permission for filming to take place in the location of a church or a centre, sometimes in our college at Stansted. Over the years I have got used to working with the media. It probably helped that I was used to taking a major part in large meetings where I knew that my words were being noted in detail and often recorded.

I remember one rather humorous meeting when a Japanese camera team were filming a meeting where Coral Polge and I were together, I think at Derby. These little men swarmed all over the place — in front of us, behind us. I was tempted to check my pockets afterwards to make sure none had secreted themselves away, out of sight. We never did see the results of that day. I hope it was good for them because they were very pleasant and complimentary about everything.

There have been some disastrous appearances of people on the television. Workers accept the challenge to work in front of magicians or before studio audiences, who are just out for a good laugh. The conditions are not right. Spirit do not have a chance to show their true power.

I went to one of the James Randi programmes recently screened by ITV, not to take part as I would never in a million years agree to appear in those circumstances, but if at all possible to put the case for Spiritualism. I spoke out as did many at what I felt was the unfair presentation. I was not shown. My protests were as nothing to this sceptical magician.

I have read of Randi's challenges to mediums and those of others like him, but would not use my gift in such a blatant attempt to make Spirit look worthless. I could have earned far more than they offer if I wished to debase my gift, to use it just to make money.

I do not object to appearing for a serious discussion or to make a point. Indeed, I encourage others to do just this, but do warn people that they must not take for granted that the producers will be on their side. I have quite a lot of people asking for interviews and always try to oblige if I think it is right.

Filming is a very expensive business. The union does not have the amount of money required as a rule. We made an exception when we held our centenary meeting at Wembley in 1990. The Publicity Committee arranged to film the events of the whole day.

Fortunately, through Mike Scott, a member of the committee, we were offered the services of someone who was an expert in making videos. Special equipment had to be hired so that the mixing could be done on the spot. This was done in such a way that although there were two cameras, the best shots were those which were recorded onto the main film. It was all very complicated.

Although this was done at cost, and we were very grateful, by the time the film had been edited down to three tapes, it had cost thousands to produce. We still sell quite a few of the number one tape — it features extracts from the day — and number two, which is of Ray and Joan Branch giving a healing talk and demonstration.

I must say, though, that the main tape is a wonderful record of different ways mediums have of working at a large meeting. It does look very professional. I insisted that the cost of the tapes be kept low so that people could afford a copy. Although this venture was expensive for us, I think it was a vital record which the union had to afford for posterity.

At the time of writing, we have had a programme made just for us for BBC 2's "Open Space." We specified the conditions of work and the content of the programme — and that is very different from just working in a studio. There was enormous public response. Six sacks of mail were delivered to the BBC asking for leaflets whilst dozens of people wrote asking for the address of their nearest church or for help.

Of course, even this was not perfect. The editor did not realise the importance of establishing the identity of the spirit communicator and in one shot, where I was demonstrating, cut out this vital moment in favour of the message. Fortunately, they were able to put this back in. We are still learning so much.

I was asked to do other radio interviews stemming from the

interest this programme, which was screened nationally, aroused. These are generally local stations. Perhaps they have a greater freedom to choose to broadcast what people want to hear.

I am pleased that now our Publicity Committee is being asked to make serious comment on psychic and spiritual matters both on radio and television. We are arranging training for some of our tutors on how to cope with media interviews.

I think this is important. It is time for us to move more into the open, just as our workers did in the larger halls so many years ago. But it must be on our terms!

One day we will break down the prejudice against Spiritualism being taken seriously as a religion and see our services broadcast in Britain.

Chapter 26

MINISTRY OF HEALING

ALTHOUGH I am not widely known as a healing medium, I have had considerable success in that field. Harry Edwards focused his faculties of physical mediumship into an energy which had effect upon the physical body of patients, but I did not do this. I felt that my gift lay mainly in proving survival. However, I have had quite good results whenever I've given healing to people.

I was always eager to have Stansted Hall used more as a centre for healing, but it never seemed to take off in that way. I seldom did any healing at Stansted, but concentrated more on my work in my own church. Most of my healing took place there in the 1950s. After that I couldn't be there as often.

Healing is part of any church work, but we were trying in all ways to improve everything that Longton church offered. I started a group to be run under my leadership. I had a very good spirit helper called Dr John, who specialised in healing and was a first class diagnostician. Frank Tams, a very dedicated medium and an excellent healing channel, was to work closely with me in this project.

I arranged that Kath Jebb would be in charge of the organisation. She was a tower of strength in our church. It is through her that I am able to recall just a few of the many hundreds of people who were helped through my healing ministry. Kath also kept all the records of the physical circle which met for years in Longton church. That was a monumental task in itself.

It was decided that Dr John would see the most serious cases. In the beginning he also gave healing, but as time went on he started to run the healing more like a clinic and only came in on special cases.

Dr John would receive patients, diagnose what was wrong and very often tell them just how they had got into that condition. He prescribed what type of healing was needed, which healer was suitable to give a particular patient healing and where the hands should be placed.

Kath recorded these instructions and would arrange it all. If Dr John wanted to see any person again, she would make an appointment. It all depended on how serious their condition was. We were always very busy, especially after people knew that the healing was being run in this way by Spirit.

In 1952 I remember a plea for help from a village about 12 miles from our church. It was from the mother of a young lady called Jean. She was unable to walk, was crippled with arthritis and also had TB. Jean was a lovely person. She had a great sense of humour, but was so frail it was pitiful to see her.

She was so young, so pretty and yet lived her life confined to a hospital type bed where there were facilities to lift her without causing her even more pain. Her mother had heard of some of the things we were doing. We were her last hope. They were a lovely family, so close and so courageous.

Frank and Kath went to visit Jean at first. For weeks, Frank gave her healing. In the end, he asked if I would go as he felt Dr John's expertise was needed. I agreed and went not once or twice, but many times in the following months.

The guides used to talk to Jean. So did Frank, Kath and I. We spoke about Spiritualism, about life after death, about the many things which are important to the spirit self. Jean seemed to have a tremendous insight and gradually gained hope of a different horizon. I never promised her she would walk again. I couldn't because I knew the eventual outcome.

I did promise that one day she would join in with a Spiritualist service. Then the time came when I realised she had not much time to go. There was part of me that was sad. Jean was so young, but had suffered so much. Even with spirit help, we couldn't change her destiny.

I decided that she would see a service, even though I had to make special arrangements for it to be in her own home. I spoke to our church members. Bill Harratt arranged some hymns whilst Frank came along and did a reading. Kath gave a short address and I a demonstration.

It was a proper service, even though there were only a few there. Some of our church people joined us along with members of Jean's family. Two weeks later, her time here on earth ended and she passed into her new home. We had become very fond of this child yet could not grieve.

There was a rather marvellous sequel to this which happened only a few weeks later. In the physical circle I held regularly in our church at that time the voice of Cuckoo was heard, saying, "I have a surprise for you."

The ectoplasm built up, and a form moved to the outside of the cabinet. A young person with a swirling gown moved gracefully and confidently out towards Kath. It was Jean!

"Look Kath," she said. "I can walk! Look at my hands!" She held out her hands. And the fingers were straight and true; those poor fingers so deformed in this life were straight and supple. Tears of joy ran down Kath's face. Other members of our circle who had not known Jean felt the emotion and responded in turn.

Jean thanked Bill Harratt for the hymns played at her own special service. She moved across the room to Sally Morgan, a member of our church who attended the service at Jean's home, thanking her for the flowers which she gave to brighten her room. Lastly she spoke to Frank. "I enjoyed your reading," she said. "Please thank Gordon. He gave me so much happiness." "May God Bless him" were her last words as she returned to the cabinet.

Of course, not all cases are so dramatic. There was lady called Marjorie who has recorded her testimonial for our records in the church where she is still a member. Marjorie was a member of the national fire service and had been discharged suffering with TB. That was in 1944. It wasn't until years later that she came to us at Longton.

We gave her healing, but were unable to clear the condition. Marjorie was readmitted to a sanatorium in Shropshire, eventually being discharged in 1965. Some six months later she had to have a complete mastectomy and radium treatment. Marjorie returned to us because she knew that the risk of secondary tumours was high and feared that her old problems might return. She was a wonderful lady, always willing to help other people and always sure of Spirit. Her testimonial ends: "I am now in my seventy-eighth year. The healing I had saved and changed my life." She is still active and healthy.

Irene was a young mother who had a nasty fall from a motor cycle. She contracted TB and severe arthritis in the legs. After healing by Frank and I there was some improvement, but not really in her legs where it was most needed. Irene asked if she could talk to Dr John. He told her he would see to her personally, assuring her she *would* dance again.

A few months later, Irene was able to return to work...and did indeed dance again. She organised a dance and donated the proceeds to a local hospital. Irene walked to work and home every day, about a mile — more than she could have managed before she came to see us at Longton. She led a full and useful life thanks to the healing power of Spirit.

Anne came to us in a wheelchair. When her husband brought her to us, she was in great pain. After a consultation with Dr John and a few weeks of personal treatment from him, she was told she would indeed walk again. It took two years for real change to take place, but she believed what the doctor had told her and came week after week for healing. Eventually, Anne did walk — and later ran her own business, owning two shops and working in one of them herself.

Not all of our cases were physical problems. In these, the healing can seem more dramatic. Mental problems may not seem as obvious, but can be just as hard for the person concerned to bear as those where there is physical pain or disability.

Minnie had a nervous condition. She could find no reason and happiness in her life. Dr John told her healing would help so she visited our clinic regularly. It was a slow process. Minnie had been told that we would also help, that she would improve and in time marry and be happy.

All this came to pass just as Dr John said. It did take some years, but Minnie was happy in the end. I am quite sure that the support which she received from all the healers and members of our church played their part in her recovery. Minnie still keeps in touch with Kath and the church.

This was another case where the patient did as much as the spirit world to help herself. Minnie could have given up because her cure took several years to become effective, but she did not. She believed what Dr John said and kept on trying.

I believe in the spirit within and know that many people can help themselves, but sometimes they need something extra. Sometimes this comes with the laying-on of hands, sometimes with the positive healing thoughts sent out, and sometimes with the strengthening of their own spiritual strength through their contact with spiritual people, both here and in the other dimension.

I realise I could have helped so many more if I had the time, but know that those that were helped had a change in their life as well as a change in their health. I often wish I had been able to do more.

Sometimes I find when visiting churches that there has been an urgent request from an old friend, and in these cases I do respond. Of course, there is always a question of time. I am so busy, but don't like to refuse when it is important. I have even been asked by my own GP to go to a patient of his who was in need.

Over the years, I've found that I have a considerable gift for absent healing. I spend quite a lot of time each day in contemplation and meditation. This is always a very good time for sending out the healing thoughts.

I do not believe in asking for things in a detailed fashion. I find it a rather odd thought that we should have to say what is wrong with a person. Healing is really of the spirit body. The etheric body will receive the power. If a cure is going to take place in the physical body, that is the first place that will be affected.

I think everyone ought to be taught about healing properly. They should, if they are directed into this form of mediumship, sit to develop the ability to link into the power of the spirit world.

I am very pleased to see how much work is now being done with the medical profession. This is a great breakthrough. I was certain it would come about, but didn't really know when it would happen. Of course, spirit healing does not emulate the doctors' work, but is complimentary to it and as such can bring such benefits to this world.

The Spiritualists' National Union was one of the founder members of the Confederation of Healing Organisations (CHO). They are dedicated to going out and working with the medical profession, thus giving a respectability to so-called alternative therapies. Of course, they do not only concentrate on healing as we define it through the Guild of Spiritualist Healers, but include all sorts of other things.

Some of these can be of immense value. I have encouraged an investigation into seeing just how beneficial they can be. I believe this is important. We must not shut our eyes to things just because we do not follow that particular practice. I have always said it is important to look at other ways.

I had healers from the Philippines at Stansted Hall two years running and have looked into the claims of others who do "psychic operations." We can do this at Stansted because we are investigating, but I always advise churches to be careful because the law of this land is quite specific. If anything went wrong, they could get involved in problems.

Once I invited Dr Alexis de Freitas from a leading London hospital together with a physiotherapist and two trained nurses to oversee the healing on a special week at Stansted. They were to observe what went on, how the healer worked and how the patient reacted, both at the time and later.

We then asked Dr de Freitas to make his comment on the results. He was not unimpressed. The healers were not versed in medical terms and did not pretend to work as doctors, but he admitted to similarities.

Of course, even now any doctor has to be careful when making comments. He felt that the patients benefited from a therapeutic effect on their minds, but would not really commit himself.

One patient, Amy Yearsley, was diagnosed by Blackpool medium Betty Wakeling as having had a brain haemorrhage. This was correct — and Dr de Freitas agreed she had more movement in partially paralysed limbs after healing. But he still felt all the improvements to which he agreed were mental rather than physical.

The event was reported in the "People" and led to thousands of enquiries. I don't know how many went to their nearest churches and were helped, but if only one person was assisted, the exercise was worth while.

I worked many times with Harry Edwards. He was superb at public demonstrations because people could see what the results were there and then.

When he started the National Federation of Spiritual Healers we were not too happy about that organisation. At one time, the union advised churches not to allow them to use our premises. The Guild of Spiritualist Healers had started by then. They naturally felt we should promote a branch of the union rather than let a different organisation take advantage of established venues.

Harry was too good a friend for the quarrel to last long. I cannot think of many who worked harder than he did on behalf of the union to raise money when we needed it so desperately.

All the member organisations of the CHO now follow the Code of Ethics which was originally devised by our Guild. Sometimes, I look at all these exams and tests and wonder just how far it will all go. Healing is a natural gift; some are more able than others. And it is not always those who pass exams who are the best instruments.

I have never taken an exam yet know that what I do works — and works well. I accept, because I have to, that this is the way of the future, and that these things are necessary. Mother would have laughed and taken no notice. She went her own way and was a marvellous healer.

Sometimes I have been asked to give healing to animals and been pleased when able to help. I remember one time when a lady approached me about her elderly poodle. This animal was very much loved, but had a heart condition. Then it dislocated a knee joint and was in agony. The vet could not help because of the heart and advised "putting her down." I was able to help — and the poodle recovered to spend more earth time with her owner.

It is not always necessary to be there to help. There was an excellent animal sanctuary at Halesowen in the Midlands. From there, a very loving lady called Mrs Hussen contacted me one day about a little Collie called Patch. He had kidney failure. The vet wanted to put him down.

Mrs Hussen called me, but I could not visit and so promised

to send out absent healing. Within two days that little dog was able to eat and drink normally. Further tests showed that his kidneys were functioning normally. The vet thought it was a miracle, but miracles are a one off experience and healing works all the time.

I have very often described and named animals in demonstrations. Often they come back and show themselves to just add that extra evidence of identity and the communicator names them for me. I have known people cry when they realise that a beloved pet is not lost forever, but will be there to love in the spirit world as they were in life. We must never underestimate the power of love.

Chapter 27

AS I SEE IT

MANY people from Orthodox religions still worry about eternal punishment for those who commit suicide so it is always good to be able to ease these worried minds. I have always thought how sad it is that those who are already feeling so helpless and hurt by this sort of death should have an extra burden to bear, the fear of their loved ones facing everlasting damnation.

I still remember a Mr and Mrs Blane of Croydon, Surrey. He was out of work and ill with a slow lingering illness which would cause added grief to his wife, whom he loved dearly. Mr Blane gassed himself.

His spirit return was an odd communication because although I did not realise it at the time, he knew no-one intimately in the hall. Mr Blane reached out into a room full of strangers to someone who he did not know very well in order to get his final message across to his beloved wife.

In his communication, he gave his name. The recipient accepted, but stated a slightly different name. This was accepted by me at the time because it seemed to be right, but later in the evening, Mr Blane interrupted another message to give his correct name and further intimate details, including the contents of the note left, his address and his wife's name.

With this further information, the correct identification was made. At the time the wife's name was unknown, but a visit to the address given confirmed even this. I do not know how she received this message, but surely there must have been relief to know he was now well.

Those who pass from this life apparently before their time,

even when they have taken their own life, are not being punished or going to face punishment. We do not have access to the whole picture: we cannot make any judgement on the success or failure in any life.

Spiritualism gives meaning. It shows you that you are not here by mistake, but that there is a purpose behind your presence in this life. That there is a Divine Law. It is this sort of thing that keeps us going. That life is not just three score years and ten, but continuous. There are many changes to life; there are many changes yet for us to meet and experience.

How nice it is to know that it goes on endlessly. We are not told how it goes on as we are not ready yet to be able to accept some of the divine and wonderful things that happen in our life. Only when we are ready can we move forward and see other things. The trouble with our world is that people have closed down upon the truth.

People think that life is just as it appears on the surface, but there is so much more. So many have come back to me to tell of how differently, if only they had known the truth, they would have lived their lives because they would have found a purpose that only death brought to them. We should know this before we pass so we can take up the threads which continue on into the other life we will live when we move into the spirit world.

I know I have been able to help thousands of people, and been able to change their lives because they know now we are not just a body, but a soul. We are spirit. We are a form. That there is a divine purpose to our lives. Perhaps some of us are born to play a greater spiritual part than other people, but I believe that all of us come with some spiritual destiny that is to play a part here in the age and world in which we belong.

We each of us will see things of the earth, indeed matters of the Spirit, according to our own experience.

Always, as the president and leader of the SNU, the largest group of Spiritualists in Britain, which is acknowledged as the Government-recognised body of Spiritualists, I have discouraged official pronouncements upon moral issues.

I do not think that such pronouncements help the individual make personal progress. We must come to certain conclusions through spiritual endeavour not through a leader saying "This is what you should believe." All too often this has been the case with religions of the past; the hierarchy decide what is right, what is moral and what constitutes sinful behaviour.

The followers of such creeds are then given the pattern on which to base their life and thought. That is not progress. It does not allow each person to grow in self and God. Over the years I have naturally come to certain conclusions about matters of the earth.

I do not pronounce. I offer conclusions on some matters which seem right to me. I worry about stating these things as absolute as I do not think anyone on the earth has recourse to the absolute truth.

We are still gathering information upon which we will base our conclusions. Those who will not think for themselves may take these to be right for them even if they are not right at this time. That is why I seldom make such statements.

I am often asked to explain whether certain things are factual or the result of ill informed teaching. Given that the following is "In my opinion," I offer these thoughts.

I find the subject of regression rather fascinating. Of course, we do not allow for reincarnation to be used as a basis for teaching in National Spiritualism. This is because it cannot be proved to reasonable satisfaction.

The fact is that once we accept the wonderful detail which can be given by spirit communicators, we can no longer completely prove reincarnation. We know some mediums have the ability to allow spirit entities to come close within their auric field and strongly to influence their mind and temporarily share memories with them.

Are these memories of when they too lived here on earth? Well, of course they are because that is how they prove their past identity. Are those who are hypnotised or induced into a state where regression takes place remembering their own experience or is there another identity being imposed upon their mind as a memory?

I do not say that regression is not true, but I wonder that it is not handled in a different way. It surprises me that so much interest is given to the life that was led on the earth and so little in where we were before the soul entered upon the earth again.

If regression were to give us this answer, I would be far more interested. If we have moved from one body straight into this, then the Buddhists are right and it is a transmigration of the soul rather than the Spiritualist teaching. Then all the communications we receive must be fraudulent!

That is not so because we have proved otherwise. I do think there are so many things we have to explore and find out about.

Spiritualism says you go into the etheric world and, while you are there, find out what the sum total of your life has meant.

You are given the opportunity to assess, as it were. To look at all the things you have learnt and some of those you did not learn. What you did with the talents you had, and what you did in caring and loving and using your life.

I think this is going to be quite an experience for some of us, especially those who concentrated upon the material things and became rich and successful, but missed all the beautiful experiences, the spiritual experiences.

There has been quite a lot written about near-death experiences. Most people agree they are very tempted to go on and generally turn back towards this life because of a sense of duty. I wonder if they have any real choice. I do not believe we decide when it is time for us to leave earth.

This would be a little difficult to prove or disprove as those who speak of these things are the ones who chose to return. If the spirit time is come, we will be taken into our next environment no matter what our decision might be.

Spiritualism is a progressive state. I believe that we are the same soul in a progressive state. I also believe that this is shown in the aura, which is consciousness itself. For those who can perceive, there are all the experiences of life, even of the past.

This is why I believe this. Over the years I have seen where children come into the world. When a child is stillborn or even aborted, he or she will come again into the same family.

It is ordained when a child should enter onto the earth for the child comes into this world for a purpose. There must be the conditions that are right for that soul: the right parents, the right conditions, the right body, even the right time.

A lady once came to me for a private interview. She had adopted two children as she was unable to carry to full term her own children and had lost two. The woman was led to adopt a child, but while at the home, another child was brought in and she realised she must take both.

Those adopted children were like brother and sister. When she came to me for a reading, I could see all this in her aura; her loss of two children and the subsequent adoption of the same two souls who had been born to women who were able to bear the foetus to term. The woman agreed all the circumstances and then showed to me a photograph of herself taken as a child and one of her adopted daughter at the same age. They could have been taken for twins.

You see, for me this proves the point. I could not know of this before she came, but it was there, in her aura. And the final proof was the photograph

There are children who are here who have been lost to this earth and have come again within the same family. I know this because I have seen it. The child will be born at the right moment for his or her destiny to be fulfilled.

I do not think for one moment that this knowledge will remove the pain of losing a beloved child or ease the knowledge of an abortion, but it can help and perhaps make some sense.

One thing I do know — and it is a matter which can bring immense comfort in the long run — is that no soul dies. This is an impossibility. There is an overall intelligence in this universe of ours.

The soul or spirit life of a child does not come into being until the child draws breath. A child or foetus which is aborted will come again because that soul is intended to have earthly experience. Very often the child will be born into the same family.

I believe that sometimes plans are made for a child to come and then it is found that the time is not right or the circumstances have changed. The spirit must withdraw until the right moment...and then the child will come. I cannot explain why this should be. I do not try. But I do know that all will happen according to a plan that I do not have access to. God does. And He will see that all things are right in the end.

It is always true to say we are entering into a new age. The evolution of culture and civilisation is categorised within ages when a certain kind of activity is predominant.

The Seventies were called the "Space Age" because of man's amazing landings upon the moon and exploration of other planets. The Eighties. What were they? Perhaps the age of hope, of a realisation of personal responsibility. We saw so many terrible atrocities and yet we also saw the beginning of disarmament and the collapse of the Berlin Wall.

Though man has advanced in scientific knowledge and technology beyond all expectation, it is true to say that this is an age in which God has been largely excluded. God's influence can be repelled as easily as it can be attracted because we have been given freewill.

Man has asserted his disastrous independence of God, which ultimately results in bloodshed and terror. Today's scientists and technologists are capable of unleashing forces against which modern society would have little chance of survival. We have seen what devastation can be visited upon our atmosphere by the unthinking and uncaring greed of a few.

Politicians constantly remind us of the threat to the world's peace by massing such forces. And yet they do little to bring a balance into this world. The rich countries have so much that they destroy food rather than pay for it to be taken to those who die of hunger.

Millions of people who have been murdered over the centuries in the names of freedom, justice and peace must look to our world from their higher state of life and wonder at the futility of it all.

Spiritualism was aroused to awaken man to his responsibilities. Spirit guides returned to give their message of love and compassion. It should be our deep rooted desire to improve the lives of all people, whatever their race, class or creed.

If we have found in Spiritualism the truth of man's purpose here in life and his relationship with the whole cosmic force of the universe, let us act now, before it is too late. Let us put aside the prejudices, jealousies and constant bickering and work in unity.

Either Spiritualism fulfils its purpose now or it goes the way of all other world religions. The way is now open for us to achieve the purpose that was begun over a century ago. Let not our pioneers' sacrifices be made in vain.

Spiritualism is the light of the world. Let this be the "Age of Enlightenment."

During the last war, spirit guides like the beloved Red Cloud and Silver Birch returned with light and knowledge. Their teachings brought comfort to thousands of grieving hearts, a new way of life and a realisation of God's love to all mankind's family.

I see our young people reaching out in desperation. They want a different way; they look for the things of the spirit in their own fashion. It is not always our fashion for we are of a different era and our earthly values were shaped in a different age.

They resort to the use of drugs to give them the illusion of happiness, of a "high." If they only knew that happiness and "high" is theirs by right, but not by mindless drug taking. Train their minds. Give them knowledge. Teach them about meditation and the glory of the spirit world. Drugs are not needed.

Sometimes in their desperation the young grasp at an ideal, but do not have the understanding to bring it into a reality for all mankind. They are selfish. But that is a fault of youth and always has been. Perhaps it is a deep rooted motivating factor to go forward into evolution.

There is common ground. That is in Spirit and in the spiritual essence that is in each person. We must seek out these values in our young and encourage them to investigate.

Today, there is a longing for a voice authoritative enough to bring together all men and women of goodwill, calling them to the great spiritual adventure of building a new world as we enter the New Age.

The door to spiritual vista will open when we allow the flow of inner impressions to break into our souls and guide our lives. When we bring the love of God and the deep inner desire to serve only God into our lives.

In this state of awareness there is inspiration from those in the spirit life. We must not fail them in their endeavour to bring the Kingdom of Heaven onto this earth.

Chapter 28

THERE IS NO END

I USED to pack 24 hours into 12, but can no longer do this. Sometimes I regret that I have to go to bed at all there is so much still to do.

Many people have asked me over the years about my biography. I would smile, and say, "Ye-es!" But finding the time; that is the difficulty. There are so many years to cover, so many stories to tell, so much of the teaching of Spirit to pass on.

After I had my strokes in 1990, I had to cut down quite drastically. I had thousands of letters and cards wishing me well. But I know how many of the SNU's centenary meetings were spoiled because people would not book as I was not going to be there.

I started back to work as quickly as possible, but was afraid. Yes, afraid. While I was so poorly, I had no spirit communication. I didn't know if I had lost it! Well, I hadn't, and I thank God. I cannot stand being idle, but love working. My dearest wish is to die in harness.

Now I still fulfil many bookings across the country, but not as many as I did. I spend much of my time now at Stansted Hall where I have been the principal for so many golden years. I see the young ones starting out, feeling their way and then surging forward. I know our future is there.

As Spiritualists, we know there is another world. We know that there is nothing supernatural, that everything is in perfect accordance with natural law. We must teach our young ones to absorb this knowledge and to use it in their work.

I often regret the passing of the old-style Lyceums. I was a member of the Lyceum from a very early age and in this found the companionship of others who were being brought up in the same beliefs as I was.

I was taught not just about Spirit but about my own self. In standing up in such company, I found confidence in doing things for other people. I learned all about service to my fellow man. I am glad that there seems to be a revival in the Lyceum movement for the young.

In my day, there were so many. Nearly every church had its own Lyceum. We used to meet and hold our own meetings. We had our flags. Some were really grand. We had a pride in our own group. We knew that only our physical body dies, that our real self goes on to the better life. But we were taught that we had a responsibility here and now to make sure that this life had meaning.

In these groups we learned we could not always like each other, but because of the spirit which joins us into a brotherhood we must endeavour to love each person we meet. That has been a tremendous help to me in life when I have had to face such difficult and sad experiences with other people.

The young are our future. If we do not take the time to train them in the ways of the Spirit, we are neglecting our own future.

After all the suffering and the bloodshed — and despite the advanced knowledge of today — the world must be seen by man to be no better or more sane. We make the same mistakes again and again, create the same conditions of hunger and want throughout the world, continually neglect our true nature to pursue a dream of avarice and power.

This must change. The responsibility for that change is ours. We cannot delay, we cannot leave this to tomorrow. We owe this effort to our children and their children. Spiritualism is a sane and rational religion. I truly believe it is the hope for mankind's future. I also believe it is the only religion which has taken change into its basic understanding.

Perhaps unconsciously people seek to find some greater crusade to achieve a more spiritual way of life. Many are turning to religious philosophies which give a feeling of security by promising that if the individual fulfils a strict programme they will be rewarded. They feel their lack of spirituality, and hope by being more severe and austere in their religious practices that they can atone. But earthly practices and a God of wrath will not change the hearts of men.

From time to time, prophets and seers have warned the world that attention must be given to the Spirit and the spiritual. They have tried to awake people to a much needed truth.

Is the cause of our world calamities to be found in our utter neglect of God and spiritual values? This question was sent to all our churches in the New Year of 1976 and is as valid now as it was then. As Spiritualists, our concern must be with the world situation. Mankind has become so dangerous to itself that the nations of the world have no alternative but to learn to embrace our principle of "The Brotherhood of Man" if he wants to avoid destruction.

The amazing discoveries of science have given man an immense confidence in his own powers. Life on this planet has been transformed in the last 70 years into a new age of advancing knowledge and technology.

In less than 60 years, man advanced from the first powered airflight to the first landing on the moon. Where were the spiritual needs of the world in all this?

Has man become all powerful and able to achieve all his needs? Indeed not. He is dependent on God. He cannot make the sun rise, flowers grow or prevent death and rebirth.

But there is an awakening. I see a hunger for a new vision of life. The door to spiritual vista will open when we allow the flow of inner impressions to break into our souls and guide our lives. When we bring the love of God and the deep inner desire to serve only God into our lives: then we will understand our relationship with all life.

In this state of awareness there is inspiration from those in the spirit life. We must not fail them.

I love mediums. That is why I go out of my way to help those whom I recognise as being sincere and honest. I try to shield them from those things which I, as a medium, have had to experience.

I do not think we are of any use to the spirit world as mediums, leaders or people to respect if we expect everything to go easily for us. We do make foes. One of the things Silver Birch taught me was that "If you do not make an enemy, then your work has not been of use to mankind."

The great guide said this to me in an hour of sorrow. I took such comfort from his words. They seemed to give a dimension to my difficulties which I had not been able to perceive. I had to stop and think more about my troubles, but in a very different way.

I have no fears for the future for we have the finest mediums with wonderful gifts. What we need now is to take the message into the highways and by ways: that God has given us the opportunity by sending ministering angels to guide us, influence us and help us through this wonderful power of mediumship.

Great guides from the spirit world have always said — and I have many writings taken from my own seances to this effect — that this great island of ours will never be the powerful nation it was in the past, but that it will be great in a different way: in teaching, in government, in our universities, in all the things we know we can do.

It is unfortunate that our governments are not guided by the spirit world but by issue, motive and purpose. In the past, great leaders went for advice from the spirit world. What a pity it is that our leaders of today do not do this, that they do not have their own guides to help them, not in political matters but in those of the Spirit. I believe this would make so much difference.

Remember all that lies ahead is there. We are sowing seeds today that will bring about vast changes in the world of tomorrow. Because some mediums are able to see the past, the present and the future together, we are able to distinguish how what we are doing today will effect those situations which are coming towards us in the future.

On one of my visits to the Silver Birch circle, I asked about the future of Spiritualism. Silver Birch told me: "The Great Spirit knows what's going on. The Great Spirit will bring in, at the right time, those who will do the work and be able to help humanity."

I have often thought of those words, and that it was a long time in coming. But to my pleasant surprise I now have those I love dearly among young people, those whom I look upon as sons and daughters. They have some remarkable gifts.

So I have lost one of my fears about passing over for I have wondered who will take on the yoke of responsibility which I have carried. I have been able to see for myself and help many of these young mediums so they do not encounter the pitfalls I did. They will go further ahead and add to mediumship for they see it in a different way than I and many others saw it in the past.

Spiritualism is religion, not a religion. I know Spiritualism's future is not to be kept just for the few, but for the whole of humanity. We must let people see the wonderful things we have experienced, not to convince but to prove why we are committed to this way. Spiritualism is so real. It has meant so much to me in my life.

Be proud that you are in the front line taking our message to the world.

For further information on Spiritualism or the SNU, please write to:

*The General Secretary,
Spiritualists' National Union,
Redwoods,
Stansted Hall,
Stansted Mountfitchet,
Essex CM24 8UD.*

Tel: 0279 816363.

Information on the Arthur Findlay College can be obtained from the manager at:

*Stansted Hall,
Stansted Mountfitchet,
Essex CM24 8UD.*

Tel: 0279 813636/7.